IMAGES
of America

ARLINGTON COUNTY POLICE DEPARTMENT

The original nine members of the newly formed Arlington County Police Department are pictured here on February 1, 1940. From left to right are (first row) C. Burns Pressley, Hugh Jones, Chief Woodyard, county manager Hanrahan, and John Saunders; (second row) Ernest Miller, Joseph Marcey, Jim East, Jack Ward, and James Scott. (Courtesy of the Arlington County Police Department Archives.)

ON THE COVER: From left to right, motor officers Raymond Crack, Vernon Wilt, Lyman King, and Babe Burke pose on Harley Davidson motorcycles in 1934 in front of the Arlington National Cemetery Hemicycle, the keystone of the grand Renaissance gateway to Arlington National Cemetery. (Courtesy of the Arlington County Police Department Archives.)

IMAGES
of America

Arlington County Police Department

Janet Rowe

ARCADIA PUBLISHING

ISBN 978-1-4671-2283-2

Published by Arcadia Publishing
Charleston, South Carolina

Printed in the United States of America

Library of Congress Control Number: 2014944690

For all general information, please contact Arcadia Publishing:
Telephone 843-853-2070
Fax 843-853-0044
E-mail sales@arcadiapublishing.com
For customer service and orders:
Toll-Free 1-888-313-2665

Visit us on the Internet at www.arcadiapublishing.com

To all faithful members of the Arlington County Police Department who have served and will serve with duty, honor, and commitment

Contents

Acknowledgments		6
Introduction		7
1.	Chiefs and Fallen Heroes	9
2.	Stations and Buildings	23
3.	Training	29
4.	Officers and Other Personnel	37
5.	Vehicles and Equipment	55
6.	Traffic and Safety Enforcement	73
7.	Specialized Units	81
8.	Significant Events	101
9.	Investigations	113
10.	Pentagon Attack Response	123

ACKNOWLEDGMENTS

I would like to gratefully acknowledge and thank all the people who assisted with this book by sharing their photographs and knowledge of departmental history with me: Kenny Adams, Bob Brown, Bruce Benson, Shirley Crack, Jim Daly, Lynn Davis, Rose Marie Dooley, Alvin Fuchsman, Clyde Hall, Dan Hartle, Barbara "Boots" Jeunette, Elwood "Woody" Hibberd, Lendel Holsclaw, Tom Hudgins, Jim Keaton, James Jenkins, Bernie Lunsford, Fran Minnich, John Mitchell, John Moore, Ernie Morris, Marty Parr, George Peever, John Quade, Ed Redenbo, W. Neil Rowe, Michael Saupp, Dick Spalding, Pete Tyler, and Eileen Williams.

Without access to the police department archives this endeavor would not have been possible, so I am indebted to Chief Doug Scott, Capt. Michelle Nuneville, Det. Christine Everest, and the Arlington County Police Association board. Extreme gratitude is extended to MPO Tara Gottsacker Crider, who assisted with the photographic scanning of images in the book. The photographs in *Arlington County Police Department* are primarily from the archives of the Arlington County Police Department, unless otherwise noted at the end of the caption crediting the contribution of private individuals and the Arlington County Public Library.

All author proceeds are donated to the Arlington County Police Department Beneficiary Association's Friends and Family Fund.

INTRODUCTION

The history of the formalized Arlington County Police Department spans a short time period of 75 years; however, law enforcement in the county precedes that time frame.

Arlington County has changed geographically several times. It was part of Fairfax County, Virginia, between 1742 and 1801. In 1788, Congress organized a new federal district called the District of Columbia and created a 10-square-mile area with land in Virginia and Maryland. In 1801, the District of Columbia was divided into counties, and the area in Virginia was called Alexandria County. Alexandria County was ceded back to Virginia in 1847, and the town of Alexandria became the city of Alexandria in the county of Alexandria. In 1920, Alexandria County was renamed Arlington County and separated from the city by the Virginia General Assembly. The name was derived from the family home of Gen. Robert E. Lee, Arlington House, which resides on a hill in the Arlington National Cemetery.

Law enforcement prior to the formalized police department were conservators of the peace, including the commonwealth attorney, sheriff, special officers, and citizen leagues. During the Civil War, the county had several fortifications, and the Union troops participated in various recreational activities, frequenting brothels, saloons, and gambling establishments. Those businesses brought with them tendencies for violence and criminal activity. The Rosslyn area was the primary place were these vices were enjoyed. The area was so bad that a ravine behind where the present-day Key Bridge Marriott hotel is located was known as "Dead Man's Hollow" for the number of bodies disposed of there.

Crandall Mackey, the commonwealth's attorney in 1904, formed a posse armed with axes, hammers, and sawed-off shotguns as a result of complaints from citizens and developers. They entered each business harboring and facilitating illegal activities and destroyed it. Attorney Frank Lyon found a clause in the liquor license that required adequate police protection before a saloon could be licensed. The sale of liquor came to an end as there was just one sheriff and a constable at the time.

Law enforcement continued to grow, and prior to 1940, the conservators of the peace were a sheriff, one deputy, 12 special officers, three justices of the peace, and one constable. They were compensated by each warrant service, arrest, or other service performed. The other work included inspecting all privies in the county, and the pay was $2 a day for privy checks. Special officers were appointed by a circuit court judge, and if they had other salaried employment, they were not compensated for their law enforcement duties.

In 1940, Sheriff Fields recommended that a police department be formed to handle the growth of the county and follow the trend of police departments as the primary law enforcement authority in jurisdictions. On February 1, 1940, Harry Woodyard, a deputy sheriff, was named the first chief of police after the county board unanimously voted for the formation of the department. The original nine members expanded to 39 by 1943. Veteran officers took evening classes to learn about police procedures, and recruits completed two weeks of evening classes. Full-time recruit classes began in 1948. This decade brought about more patrolling by vehicles, motorcycle, and "footmen" to respond to service calls throughout the developing county.

Additional residential and commercial development in the 1950s brought a variety of change to the department. The crime scene unit was established, a patrol wagon for prisoners was added to the fleet, the detective bureau was formed, and a patrol camp for youth was established. Standardized forms for incidents and traffic summons were created, and there were upgrades in the communications system. The first sworn woman was hired and assigned to the juvenile bureau.

The following decade included upgrades to cruisers; communications systems, including a teletype system allowing communications with surrounding jurisdictions; and crime scene investigation equipment. Recruits were trained by professors at American University until 1965, when the department joined with other jurisdictions at the Northern Virginia Police Academy. The first canine (K-9) unit was formed with the addition of Rommel and Lucky.

The county continued to change with the failing economy of the 1970s and the social environment brought on by the Vietnam War. Officers assisted with antiwar protestors, and a tactical unit was formed to reduce street crimes. Minority officers were hired, and in early 1973, Arlington County was the first suburban department to assign women to a patrol function.

The 1980s brought additional changes in equipment, training, and technology, making it one of the most progressive departments in the country, and in 1984, it became the first agency in Virginia and the second in the country to receive accreditation by the Commission on Accreditation for Law Enforcement. In 1989, it was the first to be reaccredited. The 911 Emergency Response System was adopted to allow for better service to the citizens. The department also set records in 1984, when it became the first jurisdiction in Virginia history to have a DNA sample submitted and accepted as evidence during a capital murder trial, resulting in a conviction.

The department responded to a changing community during the 1990s with bike patrols, community policing teams, addressing bilingual issues, and school resource officers assuming more duties within the school environment to reach the youth population.

The events of September 11, 2001, struck close to home for the department. The Pentagon, located in Arlington County, is patrolled by the Pentagon police force, but they were not equipped to handle an incident of such magnitude. Arlington police quickly took control of the situation and assisted with immediate perimeter security, victim rescues, and coordinating the traffic fleeing the District of Columbia in fear of other attacks. Members of the department spent several weeks assisting with on-scene security, evidence collection, and victim recovery.

The department is proud of its history of serving the community, and with the current force of 371 sworn and 97 civilian employees, the hope is to continue to provide a high quality of life to the citizens of Arlington County.

One

Chiefs and Fallen Heroes

Howard B. Fields was the longest-serving sheriff in Arlington County, a job he held for a total of 24 years. He was known for his tough demeanor. In 1940, Sheriff Fields recommended that a separate police department be formed and moved under the control of the county manager. Fields Park and Fire House No. 2 are located on property where Sheriff Fields and his wife resided, at the corner of Wilson Boulevard and North George Mason Drive.

Harry Woodyard became the first chief of police on February 1, 1940, when the Arlington County Division of Police was formed. Chief Woodyard was previously a deputy sheriff for Arlington County, and he was born and raised within the county and attended high school at Washington and Lee High School. He retired from the department in March 1951.

The fire and police divisions were formed into the Department of Public Safety in 1951. Carlisle Johnstone was appointed as the director, and he was in charge of the division of police following the retirement of Chief Woodyard until December 1951, when William Fawver was appointed chief. He had previously served as chief in Hopewell, Virginia, and Montgomery, Alabama.

Maj. William Fawver was appointed in December 1951 and served as chief until his retirement in June 1973. His appointment coincided with a rapid growth within the county after World War II, and under his leadership, the department grew from a force of 20 men to 285 men and women. He was instrumental in the founding of the Northern Virginia Criminal Justice Academy. Major Fawver joined the department in 1940, filing a no-experience application six months after the department was formed. During his career, he served as a motorcycle officer and a supervisor in the traffic division.

The county manager appointed Roy C. McLaren, formerly with the International Association of Chiefs of Police, as the new chief on June 1, 1973. Chief McLaren resigned in 1978 after a dispute with commonwealth's attorney, William S. Burroughs, over an investigation of a double homicide where the suspect was tried and acquitted. During his tenure, he reorganized the department by creating four divisions: operations, investigations, services, and staff. Chief McLaren had been an officer in Berkeley, California; served as an assistant chief in Dale City, California; and later organized the police force in Novato, California. He was the author of several police procedural publications. Chief McLaren was an advocate for officers' higher education, and he established a two-year minimum college requirement for applicants.

Capt. William K. "Smokey" Stover was appointed by the county manager as chief in October 1978. He served as chief until his retirement in 1996. He joined the department in 1956, became a sergeant by 1966, and was promoted to captain in 1976. Chief Stover reorganized the department into three divisions: patrol, services, and major crimes.

Following the retirement of Chief Stover, Edward Flynn (at right) was appointed chief. He launched a new era of community-based, problem-oriented policing and was at the helm during the department's response to the 9-11 attack on the Pentagon. He left the department in 2002. In the interim period, Deputy Chief Stephen Holl was acting chief until 2003.

M. Douglas Scott was appointed chief in 2003. He started his law enforcement career as a cadet with the Fairfax County, Virginia, police department in 1975 and rose in the ranks. He became their chief in 1995. In 1998, he left Fairfax County and became chief of the Fairfax City Police Department. Between 2000 and 2003, he held a position with the US Department of the Interior as an assistant inspector general.

SPO Louis Shaw was transporting a prisoner on December 6, 1935, when his vehicle was struck by a gasoline tanker on Jefferson Davis Highway and burst into flames. Officer Shaw and his prisoner were trapped in the vehicle and perished in the fire. At the time of his death, he was a court-appointed officer under the Arlington County Circuit Court. Officer Shaw had a job working as a bouncer at a local bar, and he did not earn a law enforcement salary. On April 19, 2005, the Arlington County Board passed a resolution recognizing Officer Shaw's sacrifice, and he was noted as the first officer killed in the line of duty in service to the county. The funeral for Officer Shaw was attended by members of the law enforcement community and local leaders. (Right, courtesy of the Officer Down Memorial Page, from archives of the Shaw family.)

Det. Russell Pettie was killed in the line of duty on January 20, 1954. He was attempting to serve a sanity hearing warrant. The subject barricaded himself in a bedroom with a sawed-off shotgun and pistol. The subject refused to surrender, and following the deployment of tear gas, the house was searched on the first floor. Detective Pettie exited the house, and as he turned back toward the residence, he was shot in the left temple by a round from a .30-30 rifle fired from the attic. Neighboring jurisdictions responded for assistance, and following a gun battle where approximately 7,000 rounds of ammunition were fired, the subject was killed. Detective Pettie's funeral was held with military honors at Arlington National Cemetery, with his fellow officers and those from surrounding jurisdictions in attendance.

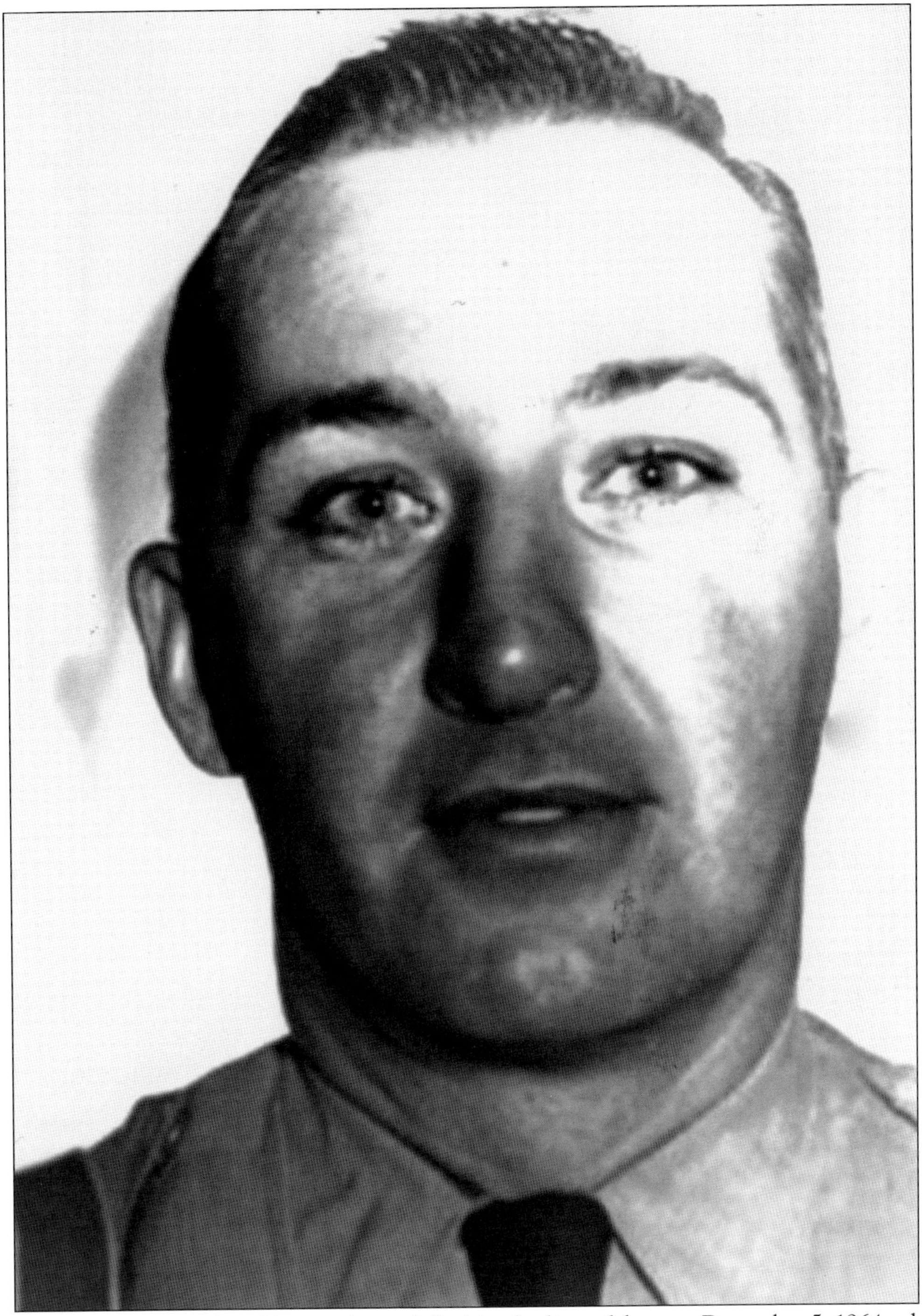

Motorcycle officer Arthur Chorovich was killed in the line of duty on December 5, 1964, when he was responding to a call to assist the fire department with a fire. He was struck by a vehicle at the intersection of North Stafford Street and Washington Boulevard. The vehicle pushed his motorcycle into the fence line at Washington and Lee High School, and he died from his injuries at Arlington Hospital. He served the department from 1951 until his death.

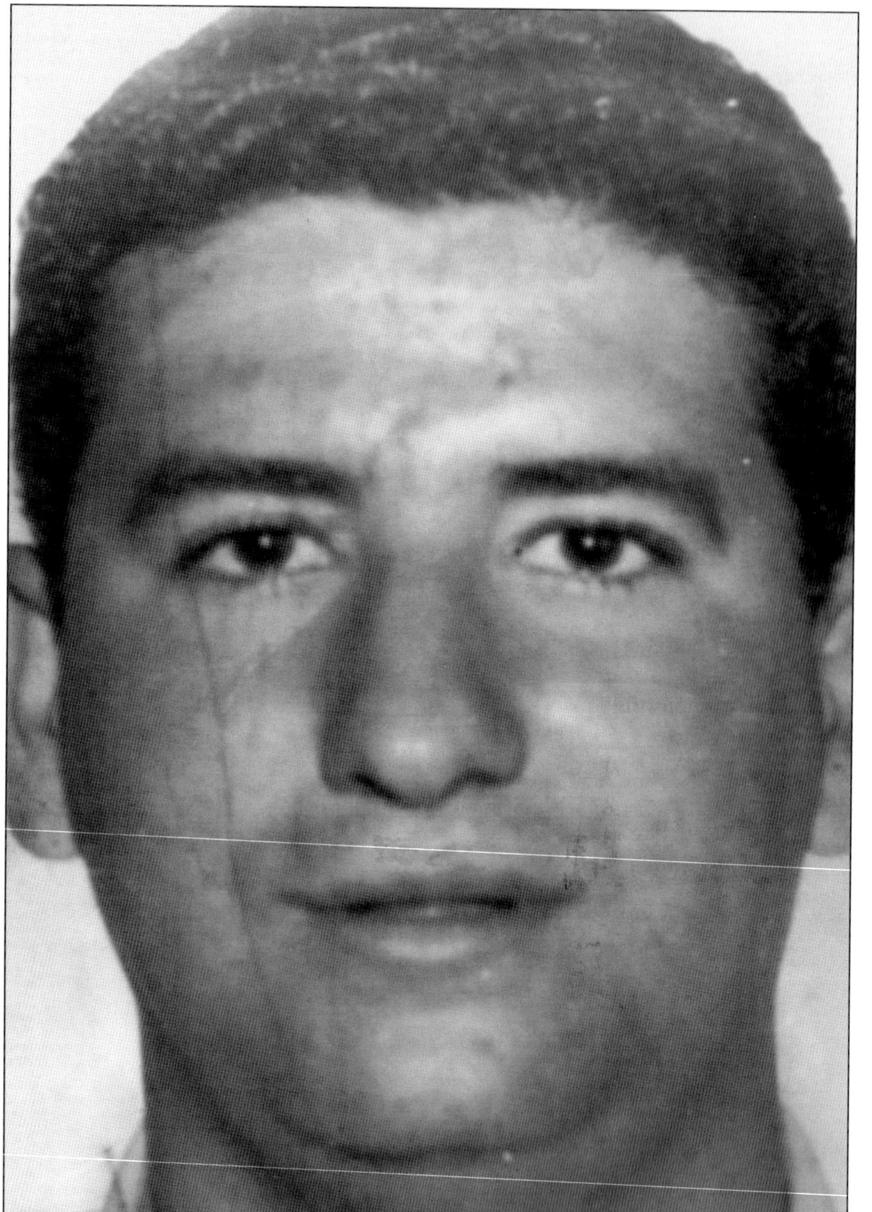

Officer Israel Gonzalez was killed during a bank robbery in Crystal Plaza on September 25, 1972. The suspects, disguised as telephone repairmen, cut the alarm and phone lines in the area. Officer Gonzalez encountered one of the suspects while performing a bank check. The suspect shot him six times in the groin, leg, and shoulders. Officer Gonzalez returned fire twice, striking the suspect. The suspects escaped, making their way to Houston, Texas, where they killed an airline ticket agent and hijacked a plane to Cuba. Their flight to Cuba invoked a 1904 pact between Cuba and the United States to extradite murder suspects; however, lengthy negotiations facilitated through the Swiss embassy with Cuba to have the subjects returned failed. Three of the suspects, Charles, Bryce, and Jonathan Tuller, returned to the United States and surrendered in 1975. William Graham surrendered in 1992. It was determined that Officer Gonzalez had shot Bryce Tuller twice in the hand.

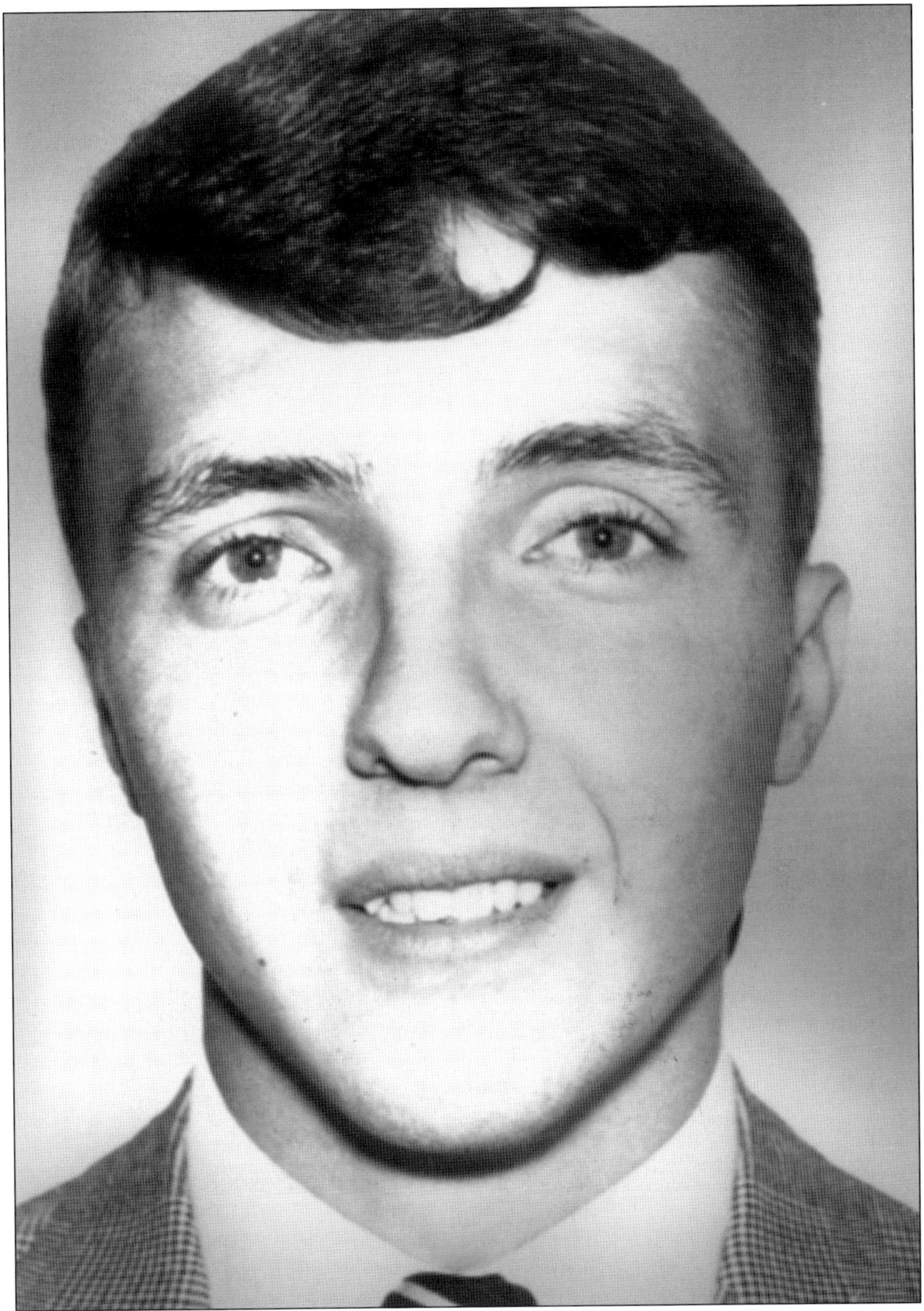

Officer George Pomeraning was killed on September 2, 1973, transporting a prisoner that he and his partner arrested for appearing to be under the influence of drugs. The subject had struggled during the search, making a search of his person difficult. Officer Pomeraning was sitting with the suspect in the back seat of the cruiser when the suspect pulled a gun from his boot and shot him three times, killing him instantly. His partner, Gerald Dawson, was wounded during the incident. The incident led to the department implementing periodic continuing education courses on search and arrest procedures.

On April 15, 1977, officer John Whiteoak Buckley was shot and killed responding to a silent alarm at the Virginia National Bank located at Columbia Pike and South Glebe Road. Officer Buckley confronted one of the robbers as he exited the bank and was taking him into custody when a second suspect approached from behind and shot him. It is believed that the suspects were escaped prisoners from another state and part of a robbery ring. The suspects are serving life sentences on other charges.

Every May 15, designated as Peace Officer Memorial Day by Pres. John F. Kennedy in 1962, the department holds a memorial service for the officers killed in the line of duty during National Police Week. Other agencies are in attendance as evidenced by deputies from the Arlington County Sheriff's Department standing on the steps. Honor guards from the sheriff's office, Fairfax County police, and Alexandria police present the colors during the ceremony. Auxiliary officer Charles Neal reads the names of Arlington's fallen as Lt. Robert Medairos salutes. Deputy Chief John Haas is to the right of Lieutenant Medairos. Behind Officer Neal, to his left is officer John Kelleher, and to his right is Cpl. Charles Brown. Arlington officers work specialized details during National Police Week, honoring all fallen officers by sending the honor guard to the National Law Enforcement Memorial ceremony at the Memorial Wall in the District of Columbia and the ceremony on the Capitol grounds. Motor officers provide escorts for the fallen officers' families and coworkers. Other officers assist the Concerns of Police Survivors organization with various programs during the week.

The department raised funds, and a memorial designed by officer Timothy Freeman to honor the department's fallen officers was dedicated on May 26, 2005, located on the plaza in front of the station at 1425 North Courthouse Road. The statue was modeled after retired officer Clyde Embrey. Bronze plaques with the likenesses of the officers and a brief history are displayed on the front. During the ceremony on National Peace Officers Day, 28 officers that died from other causes are recognized. Below, Cpl. Charles Brown (left) and officer John Kelleher (right) are members of the honor guard. Corporal Brown is a third-generation officer; his grandfather Leonard Brown Sr., grand-uncles Arthur Brown Sr. and William Brown, and uncles Robert Brown and Leonard Brown Jr. served with the department. Cpl. Beth Brown Lennon, a cousin, also carries on the tradition of service.

Two

STATIONS AND BUILDINGS

In the 1940s, there was no dedicated police department building. The officers worked out of space in the courthouse building (left) on North Courthouse Road and the old jail (right) on North Fifteenth Street.

The old jail, located at the corner of North Fifteenth Street and North Uhle Street, became the police property room and motor shed for the motor units to house their motorcycles. The ramp helped facilitate getting them into the building. The property room was accessed through a doorway in the area covered by the porch roof. Found bicycles were stored next to the building. The building to the right at 1425 North Uhle Street housed the department's communication, investigation, and patrol divisions. During the 1970s, a new jail and police department building were constructed at the intersection where the old jail and department used to be. The 1970s-era building was demolished in the late 1990s, and the jail and the police department moved to 1425 North Courthouse Road. There is a parking lot where the old buildings stood.

The old portion of the jail that had housed prisoners was demolished to allow an addition to the courthouse. Pictured here are the bars on the exterior windows as well as the barred area on the interior door where jailers would pass food to the prisoners. Prior to demolition, the prisoners' area was used by the motor unit for motorcycle storage.

In 1961, expansion to the courthouse required the department to move to another location, 1424 North Uhle Street. The radio dispatch communication center was located on the first floor, and the radio frequency KIB-346 is visible on the front window. The communications center was upgraded with control panels for burglary and hold-up alarms and one for monitoring officers' locations.

Pictured here around 1961 is the old jail, when it was utilized as the police property room. The building was demolished the same year for the construction of the new courthouse complex. Officers Hamilton Creasy (left) and Robert Jones (right) worked as property control officers. As is the case today, the property room stores found property as well as evidence recovered from crime scenes.

In the 1950s, the department had its own building at 1425 North Uhle Street. Several divisions of the department were housed here, including the administrative bureau, juvenile bureau, detectives, communications, traffic safety, and operations. Sgt. Harvey Barnett, assigned to the administrative bureau, is seen behind the main counter in 1952. The administrative bureau was responsible for collecting fines, report keeping, and criminal records. A major change for the department was the use of standardized forms for collecting information of incidents, accidents, and tickets. Communications is the enclosed area to the right with a teletype machine next to it.

Construction of a new jail complex in 1974 at the intersection of North Fifteenth Street and North Uhle Street included space for the police department. The jail complex was attached to the upper right, three-story section of the courthouse building. The old courthouse building (center of the photograph), constructed in 1898, had been demolished and replaced with a more modern structure in 1960. That building was then imploded on February 23, 1997.

The police department moved into its new building (right) in 1995. The building is shared with the courts system and the administrative offices of the sheriff's department. The detention center is housed in the building to the left. The parking lot is the location of the two previous courthouses.

Three
TRAINING

In 1952, recruits participate in a physical training self-defense class. Military police officers were also included in the training sessions. On the mats are, from left to right, Walter Bell (standing), George Turpin with William Hall across his back, Frank Palmer (instructor), Richard Clark, and Bill Jeunette (instructor). Among the observing trainees pictured on the hill are Robert Jones, James Connors, ? Davis, ? Mathos, ? McLaine, ? Clemens, ? Hardy, ? Bamman, ? Brown, Henry Hite, and Walter Hughs. (Courtesy of Barbara Jeunette.)

The academy's driver training course in the 1960s was a cone course in a parking lot at Potomac Yards in Alexandria. The coal-burning power plant built in 1949 in Alexandria City is in the background. Officers maneuvered through the cones to practice driving at different speeds without knocking over the obstacles. The cruisers were white with blue reflective lettering instead of solid black and were equipped with a dome light, siren mounted on the hood, air-conditioning, and the most up-to-date high frequency two-way radios. Recruits in May 1962 were also trained on driving simulators in a classroom setting. Officer Bill Jeunette is the instructor standing in the rear. Recruits are, from left to right, (first row) J. Tavarres (Vienna police), Robert Brown, and Curtis Solem; (second row) John Kinney, Chuck Gavin, Phil Nielson, and Swanson Dowling; (third row) Thomas Childrey, Quentin Thompson, Harry Hittle, and Kenny Adams.

Rookies, driving to the right above, were trained to operate motorcycles by senior officers. They are, from left to right, Sgt. Ray Cornett, Lt. John Kadel, Chief William Fawver, and officer Bill Jeunette. This training session was held at Utah Park in Fairlington, Shirlington Circle. Shirley Highway (I-395) is seen in the background, as is the Washington Gas and Light Company building next to the highway. Motorcycle helmets had not been adopted as safety equipment, and they did not become standard-issue equipment until the late 1950s.

Above, recruit officers are enjoying motorcycle training in Utah Park in the Fairlington section of the county in 1952. Below, the group assembled for a class photograph. Motorcycle training is no longer a training requirement for recruits; only officers that have requested and are assigned to the squad go through training.

Firearms training in the 1950s took place at a gravel pit in Alexandria. Officers were required to qualify with their weapons every six weeks, and they had to shoot from various positions and distances. Sgt. Ernest "Pinky" Summers is the range instructor during this firearms qualification course. In the 1960s, the firing range used by the department was a 50-foot indoor range located at Washington and Lee High School, on the 1300 block of North Quincy Street. Training was relocated in 1965 to the old Nike missile site in Fairfax County on Popes Head Road. During the 1980s, training was at a facility run by Alexandria police on Eisenhower Avenue. Arlington continued to use that range until 2008, when the training was moved to the range used by the Washington Airport Authority police at Dulles Airport. An attempt was made in 1973 to have an indoor range in the department's building at 2100 North Fifteenth Street; however, the ventilation was poor, and it was too small.

In 1965, recruit training became a joint venture with other jurisdictions when Arlington joined with Alexandria, Fairfax County, Fairfax City, and Herndon to form the Northern Virginia Police Academy on 10 acres of land in Fairfax County on Popes Head Road, at an old Nike missile site. Sgt. Joe Heath (left) was the Arlington firearms instructor at the firing range. The academy would later move to an old elementary school at 10209 Little River Turnpike in Fairfax City, but firearms remained on Popes Head Road. The 1980s found the academy relocating again to another elementary school in Arlington, Claremont Elementary. In the 1990s, a newly dedicated building in Loudoun County became the new Northern Virginia Regional Criminal Justice Academy.

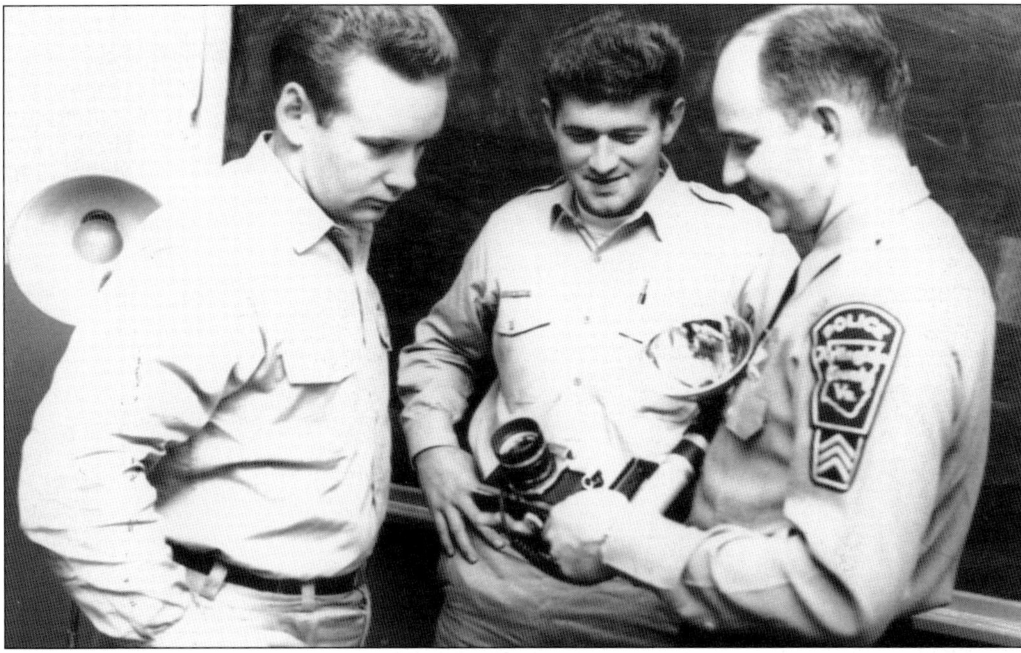

In 1966, recruit officers Leo Long (left) and Paul Cope receive instruction from Sgt. Walter Shoup on the operation of photographic equipment used to record crime scenes. Recruit officers in training receive instruction on evidence collection and record keeping to familiarize themselves with what to look for at crime scenes for the evidence technicians to collect.

Defense tactics courses to train officers to subdue belligerent, aggressive subjects were part of the curriculum at the academy. Recruit officer Rodney Mull flips recruit officer Stew Pell during a training exercise. Defense tactics are still an important part of training at the present-day academy, and officers are required to re-train on a regular basis.

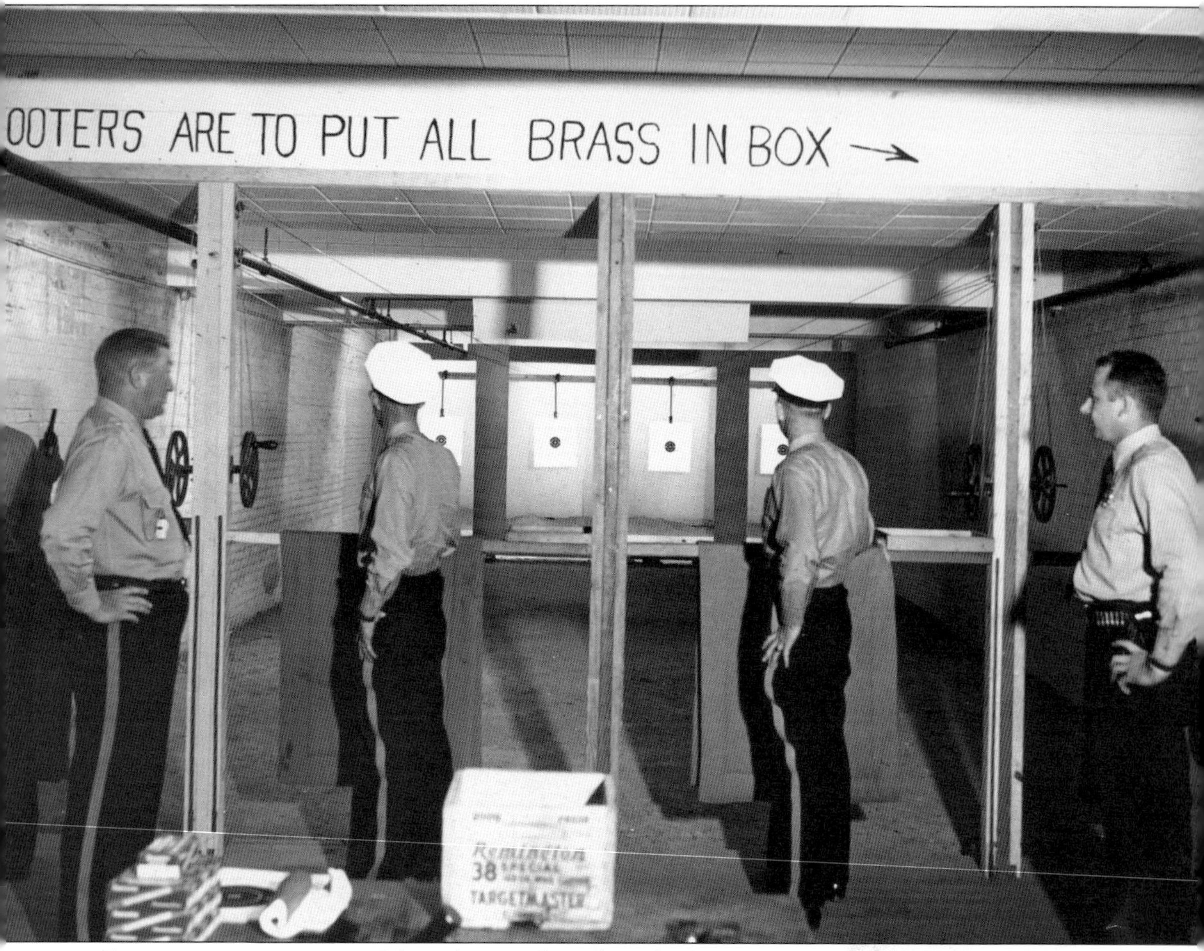

Firearm training was moved from the gravel pit along the Potomac River in Alexandria to the 50-foot indoor range at Washington Lee High School from 1950 to 1965. The range was primarily used by the high school's rifle team. The targets would move back and forth on a crank pulley system. The sign to put brass in a box was a reminder to officers to pick up their spent bullet casings.

Four

Officers and Other Personnel

Before the actual formalization of the department in 1940, the protection of the county was under the purview of the sheriff's police lead by Sheriff Howard B. Fields. Members pose in front of the old jail in 1929; from left to right are Sheriff Fields, Jack Conway, Archie Richardson, Jim East, Hugh Jones, John "Babe" Burke, Ray Cobean, and Raymond "Ox" Crack.

Officers assembled in 1931 before the old courthouse are, from left to right, (first row) Archie Richards, Ernie Miller, Vernon Wilt, John Burke, and Jack Conway; (second row) Sheriff Howard Field, Louis Elliott, Ed Duncan, H.E. Mason, Jack Conway, and William Brown; (third row) Joseph Marcey, Norman Carson, Hugh Jones, and Raymond Crack. Approximately 60 years later, the motor squad poses with Pres. George H.W. Bush. From left to right are Bruce Bartleson, Sgt. Bruce Hackert, Bruce Silvernale, Adam Stone, Gary Thorne, Lt. Richard Alt, Mike Robinson, Bush, auxiliary Charlie Neal, Sgt. Kevin Reardon, Richard Cox, Mick Wenmoth, Cpl. Karen Herchenroder, and Mark Guenther. The unit assists in providing motor escorts for motorcades escorting the president or other dignitaries. (Below, courtesy of officer Adam Stone.)

Officers pose in front of the Fairfax-Alexandria Building Association in 1936. In the front is Sheriff Howard Fields, and from left to right are (first row) Leland Gaines, High Jones, Joe Marcey, Norman Carson, Harvey Barnett, Harold Mason, James Scott, Archie Richards, John Burke, Bill Brown, and Harry Woodyard; (second row) Odie Howell, Jack Conway, Jack Cullins, Ed Duncan, Ernest Miller, Jack Ward, and Louis Elliott.

In 1932, Sheriff Fields poses with other members of the department; they are, from left to right, Jim East, Joe Marcey, Vernon Wilt, Sheriff Fields, Ernest Miller, Raymond Crack, and John Burke. The vehicle at left is marked Arlington County Police Department, even though the department was not officially formalized.

Pictured here are the sheriff's police in 1939, the year before the county board formalized the department. Motor officers wore knee-high boots, and the uniform was a blazer jacket cinched at the waist with a belt. Firearms were secured in a holster worn outside of the blazer and secured with an over-the-shoulder strap that went across the chest. The officers are, from left to right, (first row) Harvey Barnett, Douglas Topley, Raymond Crack, Howard Fields, Ed Duncan, Harold Mason, Dick Langley, and Archie Richards; (second row) Hugh Jones, Jack Conway, Ray Cobean, James Scott, Ernest Miller, Norman Carson, and Joe Marcey; (third row) Vernon Wilt, Jim East, Bill Brown, John Murray, C. Burns Pressley, Louis Elliott, Odie Howell, and John Sanders; (fourth row) Jack Ward, Harry Hunt, Harry Woodyard, Claude Barnes, Jack Cullins, Lyman King, and Leland Gaines.

By 1941, one year after the department was formed, the uniform had changed significantly. The cinched blouse-style jacket with the crossover holster strap was gone, except for ceremonial occasions, and officers wore long-sleeved light blue shirts. Hats and ties were still worn on a regular basis. The department continued to increase in size with many new officers signing on. Several of the officers in the 1941 photograph above transferred into the formalized department. Chief Woodyard is seen on the far left of the photograph taken in front of the old courthouse. The 1946 photograph below was also taken in front of the old courthouse. William Fawver, first row, fourth from right, would become chief in 1951.

Officers would attend roll call and receive their beat assignments; note the beat map hanging on the wall. Supervisors at the back are Ray Carr (left) and Lt. Joe Marcey (right). Officers are, clockwise from left, (left table) Leroy Rasmussen, three unidentified, Raymond Pope, and Joe Kane; (right table) Joe Partesi, Leonard "Tut" Brown, unidentified, Frank Keyes, Floyd Bedell, and unidentified.

Pictured here is roll call in 1952; officers line up and are inspected by Lt. Raymond Cole (left) and Lt. Raymond Carr (right). The officers were inspected for their professional appearance and whether or not they had the necessary authorized equipment with them. Patrol officers wore light blue shirts, and supervisors above the rank of sergeant wore white, long-sleeved shirts.

In the summer of 1947, the department assembles outside the courthouse. From left to right are (left side, first row) J. Kadel, Carson, Huber, Coppage, Bayliss, Reeve, W. Kadel, Benton, Kane, and Weekley; (left side, second row) Liptrap, Adams, Pettie, R.W. Keyes, Cullins, Bushong, and Wise; (left side, third row) Wanner, Mason, Captain Miller, Sergeant Cole, Sergeant Smith, Sergeant Frederich, Lieutenant King, Bell, and West; (center, first row) Jones, unidentified county manager, and Chief Woodyard; (center, second row) Palmer, Elliott, Langley, Conway, James, and

F. Keyes; (center, third row) Sanders, A. Brown, Serafin, and Hager; (center, fourth row) Smoots, Connor, Pressley, B. Keyes, Crissman, L. Brown, Barber, Rector, Franklin Runyon, Pickett, Willet, Clayborne, and Arthur; (right side, first row) Summers, Dinsmore, Stream, Hammer, Topley, Griffith, and Redmon; (right side, second row) Barnett, Lunsford, Lucas, Dodson, Heath, Perry, and Carr; (right side, third row) Boone, Fawver, Berry, and Fowler.

The recruit class of October 1957 included the first sworn female officer, Delores Brown (first row, center). She was assigned to the youth bureau. Prior to her hiring, Doris Beiswanger was hired in 1951, but it is believed that she was not sworn in and was assigned to the juvenile bureau as a matron. Academy classes at the time were held in the basement of Firehouse No. 9 at 1900 South Walter Reed Drive, and the class posed in front of the building. The recruits were sworn in following the completion of their training. Below are, from left to right, (first row) Robert Forker, Robert Gillis, John Baird, Kenneth Starnes, Kenneth Bowles, and Raymond King; (second row) Otto Koch, Dolores Brown, Frank Broadkorb, and Jessie Wismer; (third row) David Bratton, Jim Stone, Walter Shoup, Ernie Morris, Jasper Brannan, and Lewis Norris.

Alvin Fuchsman (center) held the position of unofficial police artist. Sergeant Fuchsman compiled witness descriptions of suspects in composite drawings, which were then distributed to patrol officers and detectives. While in the detective bureau, he designed a light board to show locations of cruisers assigned on calls. The shoulder patch depicting the outline of Arlington County in use from the 1950s until 1998 was one that he designed. His patch was replaced by a more colorful patch depicting a stylized depiction of Arlington House, Robert E. Lee's home in Arlington Cemetery. From left to right are Bernie Lunsford, Alvin Fuchsman, and ? Clayborne.

In the mid-1960s, Fuchsman designed a new hat shield and badge that is still in use by the department. The design is copyrighted and cannot be duplicated by other agencies. The department has issued several specialized badges to commemorate certain events: anniversaries, presidential inaugurations, 9-11, Police Memorial Wee, and a 75th anniversary badge that will be a reissue of the original 1940s design. The badges in the 1940s had badge numbers; however, the 1960s design does not reflect the change from badge numbers to administrative numbers issued to county employees. The 1940s design is pictured in the upper left and lower right. The newer badge is lower left and top right. Captain Fuchsman's patch is at the top, and it had gold embroidery for supervisors and white for patrol officers. The current patch, designed in 1998, is below it.

James "Jimmie" Jenkins became the first police cadet with the department in May 1961. The position was part of Wakefield High School's diversified occupation program. Students would receive apprentice training for jobs while they finished school. The program allowed the cadet to train through different sections of the department until reaching the hiring age of 21. Art Spedden and John Moore were other cadets that joined the department. James Jenkins was congratulated as a newly appointed cadet by Chief Fawver in 1961, and in February 1971, ten years later, Chief Fawver promoted him to sergeant. Jenkins retired from the department with the rank of lieutenant.

Police dispatcher Henry Willet received a call from two frantic women that claimed two bats were chasing them around their house at 2320 North Kentucky Street. Officers William Jeunette (left) and John Nesbitt took the two perpetrators into custody.

Members of the department are often called to handle a variety of animal-related calls. These calls consist of dog menacing, deer that have collided with vehicles, raccoons, bats, squirrels in residences, snakes, and the occasional alligator. In the late 1950s, officer George Dooley observes a scaly suspect. (Courtesy of Rose Marie Dooley.)

Animals continue through the decades to attract a police response. Here, officer Hugh Black takes a horse into custody during the 1950s, reflecting the still-rural nature of several areas of the county. This culprit in the 1960s was a raccoon, corralled by Bob Roof (left) and John Kinney (right), that was creating havoc for a homeowner.

In early 1973, Arlington became the first jurisdiction in the suburbs around Washington, DC, to assign female officers to patrol duties. Officer Ruth Ridgley, one of those first officers, is pictured above directing traffic. The first two female officers assigned to patrol were Marcia Kinkead and Betty Ann DeCamara. The women were assigned uniforms similar to the male officers, so that the public would view the same image of authority regardless of gender, but their uniforms had to be tailored. July 14, 1974, brought unrest within the department when the officers picketed the courthouse protesting an eight percent cost-of-living raise given by the county board instead of 10.8 percent, based on local increases. They also stopped writing tickets, issuing warnings instead. (Left, courtesy of Center of Local History, Arlington County Public Library.)

This 1961 recruit class swearing-in photograph in the court clerk's office reflects the absence of female recruits. The recruits are, from left to right, (first row) Arthur Chorovich, Jackson Bullock, Paul "P.J." Lewis, Richard "Dick" Spalding, Howard Dent, and Carl Tucker; (second row) Floyd Runner, Clyde Hall, Earl Huff, Joseph Bunch, Marcel Levavasseur, and Elwood "Woody" Hibberd.

The hiring of female officers increased thought the 1980s and 1990s as evidenced in this evening squad photograph from 1997. From left to right are (first row) Cpl. Steve Smith, Lt. Steve Holl, Cpl. Linda Harmsen, and Sgt. Ed Chapman; (second row) Joseph "Matt" Mitchell, Adrienne Phiel, Michele Saupp, Anita Capitello, Kamran Afzal, and John Rizik; (third row) Dave Hibberd, Damon Washington, Tom Trumble, Corey Hoggatt, Don Spears, and Janet Rowe; (fourth row) Jeff Swanson, Barbara Hale, Joe Kantor, Don Fortunato, Matt Heimberger, and John Ritter; (fifth row) Cecil Mobley, Henry Buchhofer, Tom Binckley, Kip Malcolm, Mark DiGeronimo, Doug Johnson, Donald Grinder, Tamara Celestini, and Joe McGrath. The uniform shirt and the stripe on the pants changed from a light blue to a grayish blue in 1998. Officers also were allowed to wear black turtlenecks under the shirt or navy blue sweaters for comfort in colder weather.

Five

VEHICLES AND EQUIPMENT

The Plymouth Fury was the most-sold police vehicle in the United States, Mexico, and Canada in 1968, and Arlington was one of the jurisdictions that used those cruisers. The cruiser had a rotating red bubble light on top of the siren mounted to the roof, and the cars were equipped with air-conditioning, an important addition with the humidity in the summer.

The uniformed patrol section in the 1940s was divided into three sections: scout car patrol, footmen, and motorcycle patrol. There were four scout cars patrolling the county; officer Truman Adams was assigned to one of those vehicles, a 1948 Plymouth seen above on Route 7 (King Street), with the Fairlington neighborhood on the hill in the background. Below, two unidentified officers in the 1950s were found sleeping in their cruiser. Officers patrolled in two-man cruisers and worked a six-day 48-hour week. Officers caught sleeping were given a 10-day suspension; that information was published in the local newspaper. Cruisers were equipped with a two-way radio, red dome light, and a fender-mounted siren that often froze in the winter. Officers used road flares or a sheaf of burning paper to melt the ice.

The Plymouths and Harley Davidsons that made up the department fleet in the 1950s are displayed here along with, from left to right, Tom Blake, Capt. Dudley Rector, Stuart Crickenberger, Capt. Robert Weekley, Sgt. Charles Wood, Bill Jeunette, and Lt. John Wise. Below, officer John Quade, assigned to the youth resource section, is at patrol camp with his 1961 Ford 300.

In 1958, the cruiser scout car had an equipment box in the trunk. The foot locker included an accordion folder with required forms, a first aid kit, a battery-operated portable light, flares, a tarp, rope, a fire extinguisher, a clipboard, and a prisoner restraint chain. Today's cruisers are equipped with ballistic shields, and flares, and some have spike strips to disable vehicles during pursuits by flattening the tires. The vehicles also have video cameras and computers to run subject and vehicle checks, receive dispatched call information, and write reports.

Cruiser appearance changed in the 1970s. The 1974 Ford Torino has limited markings. The 1978 Chevrolet Nova was redesigned with additional reflective decals to make the cruisers more visible. The non-emergency phone number was added to the trunk as an educational tool, and the doors had the Arlington County logo design with the stylized rendering of the Lee-Custis House in Arlington National Cemetery. The emergency light bars on both vehicles were red, and the sirens were placed in the front grill. The fleet used by the department in 1971 is displayed below by, from left to right, unidentified, Ed Redenbo and Lucky, Chris Burris, and John Sarafinas. The scooters were used in shopping areas and throughout the park and bike trail system.

Prisoners were transported in paddy wagons or patrol wagons until the 2000s, when most of the cruisers in the fleet had a metal and Plexiglas screen installed between the rear passenger compartment area and the front of the cruisers, enabling transport of prisoners by the arresting officer. The 1971 version of the patrol wagon had prisoners housed in the rear box area sitting on metal bench seats running the length of the interior wall. Male prisoners were not transported at the same time as female prisoners to avoid complaints. The patrol wagon was furnished with a two-way radio, emergency lights, and a siren. The department still uses a patrol wagon, but it is primarily for mass arrests or to accommodate a prisoner of a larger stature.

In the 1940s, the identification unit had an assigned Chevrolet that transported the tools necessary to complete evidence collection. The equipment included portable lighting devices, axes, shovels, saws, collection containers, photography equipment, and fingerprint recovery tools. The vehicle had a ladder attached to the exterior of the vehicle and a platform on top for an officer to stand and process scenes that were above ground and not easily accessible.

During the 1960s, another vehicle was purchased to provide assistance for uniformed officers to gather evidence at crime scenes. The van was equipped with the tools necessary to locate, collect, and preserve evidence and had a work area in the interior. The vehicle's 2,500-watt floodlights powered by a generator could light up crime scenes or roadways to assist with accident investigations. The exterior roof had a platform for photography.

The 1990s and 2000s found the department using the Ford Crown Victoria as the standard patrol vehicle. The decal was changed to the two-tone stripe to match the shirt and pants colors of the issued patrol uniform. The decal is reflective to light and displays a replica of the badge. The emergency light bar is a change from only red to the addition of blue. The light bar later was changed to all blue. The blue makes the vehicle more noticeable when activated and is a safety feature. The piece of equipment displaying the speed limit sign is a stationary device that is set up along roadways to make drivers aware of the posted speed and how fast they are traveling. The box portion contains a radar device, and the speed traveled is digitally shown.

Communications in the 1940s required officers to call into the station from phones at homes or businesses, as there was no direct communication by radio. The first radio equipment consisted of receivers installed in the cruisers. When a call came in, the station clerk relayed the information to the District of Columbia Metropolitan police, who then relayed the information to the officers in Arlington. Communication improved in the 1950s with a 250-watt FM transmitter and receiver and a 50-watt emergency set, which expedited response times and created a safer environment for the officers. Motor officers originally had no radio contact with the station and had to constantly make phone calls to be dispatched to calls. Portable radios eased that problem, and officer Roxy Crack demonstrates the first portable radio in front of 1425 North Uhle Street. The units were extremely heavy and cumbersome compared to the small handheld units worn on the utility belt today.

Further improvement in communications came about in the 1950s. Officers assigned to dispatch duties are pictured here in the booth located in the building at 1425 North Uhle Street. Calls were dispatched on two-way radios to 15 motorcycles and 31 cruisers. Dispatchers recorded the type of call, location, date, time, and complainant information. The teletype operator visible to the right of the booth provided contact between 13 states on the East Coast. Below, officer Henry Willet is taking a call within the communications booth, where he handled the phones, fire control, and criminal booking procedures as well as dispatching officers on calls for service.

Communication is an extremely valuable component in law enforcement, both for having calls dispatched for service and ensuring the safety of the officers. Prior to 1970, contact was limited by the number of radio channels. One channel was used, and if calls backed up or if the channel was being used, other officers could not be contacted. The new system, leased for $5,650 per year, utilized a six-channel system. Two channels were assigned to uniformed patrol, two for detectives, and the remainder for such uses as coverage of large demonstrations or evolving events. Portable radios that could be clipped to the utility belt allowed officers to communicate away from their vehicles. The communication center allowed dispatchers, now civilian employees, to monitor the location of officers on calls, handle pending calls for service, and record radio calls. The dispatchers pictured here are Chuck Harris (left) and Tom Bell (right).

Communications for the county is a joint operation to cover police and fire dispatch. After the old police department at 2100 North Fifteenth Street was demolished, the Emergency Communications Center moved to a floor of the building located at 1400 North Uhle Street. The center featured individual cubicles with monitors, where dispatchers were assigned a specific channel for fire dispatch, primary police dispatch, and a police administrative channel. Call takers entered the calls for service by computer, and it was sent to the primary dispatcher for dispatch over the radio to officers. Jeff Horowitz is monitoring the primary police channel and is responsible for dispatching officers on calls. Communications personnel also are responsible for entering people, vehicles, and items into the state and nationwide law enforcement system through teletype. The communications center moved again on May 20, 2008, when a state-of-the-art communications system was installed within the new police building at 1425 North Courthouse Road.

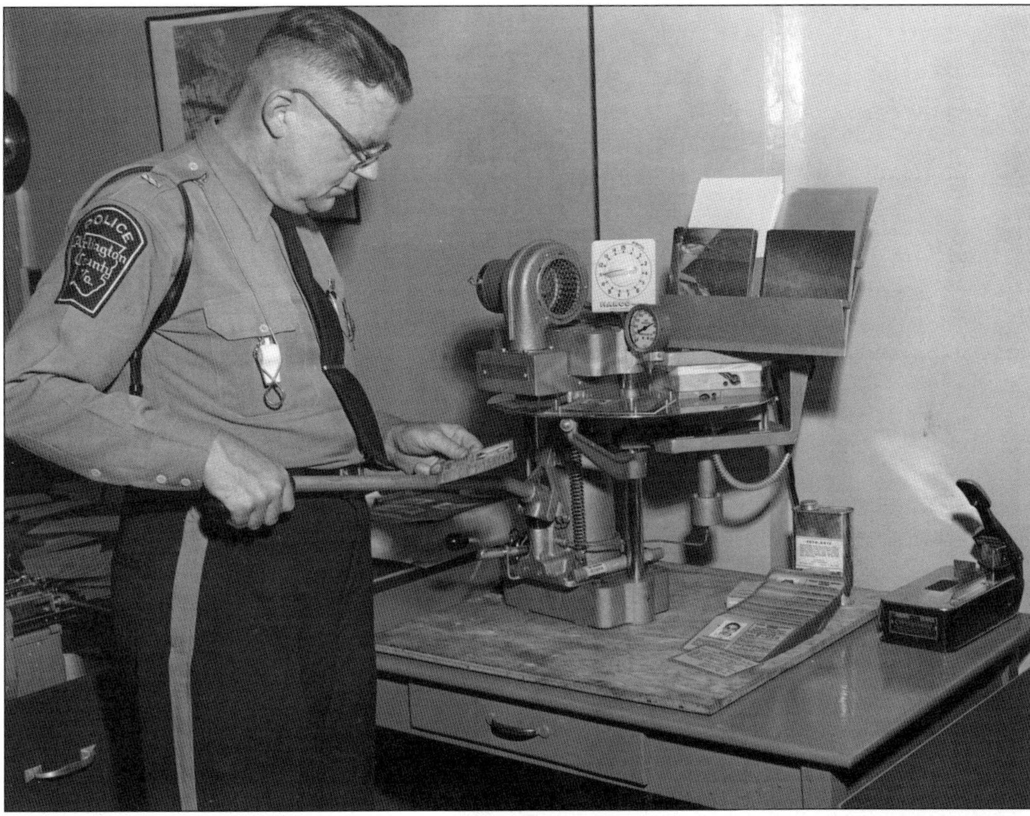

Part of the responsibilities of the department is to administer tests to individuals applying to be cab drivers and issue their taxi cab licenses. Lt. Andrew Bayliss, in charge of the licensing bureau, is making the licenses in the 1960s. The licenses seen stacked on the table have not changed over the years; however, the laminating machine has become more streamlined.

The first speed radar was invented in the 1950s by rally car driver Maurice Gatsonides to improve his racing time. He then founded a company that developed radar for use with traffic enforcement. After passing many stages of development and legal testing, radar was introduced in Arlington as a reliable method of speed enforcement. The Speed Watch radar machine is being operated by an unidentified captain.

Evidence collection and identification are essential components of law enforcement necessary to secure convictions of suspects. Clayton E. Keys, a dactylographic technician (fingerprint examiner) assigned as a civilian employee in the identification unit, utilizes a magnifier to compare the whorls and ridges on an individual's fingerprint card. Technicians often received training from the FBI. The close proximity of the bureau and their laboratory facilities created a perfect arena for the department to rely on their expertise in learning new methods of evidence collection. Below, in 1953, Lt. Andrew "Bus" Bayliss observes as an FBI technician indicates blood stains on a woman's shoe in the serology section. Lieutenant Bayliss attended the 52nd session of the FBI National Academy. The department still sends supervisors to attend the academy and learn the most up-to-date methods in a myriad of law enforcement areas.

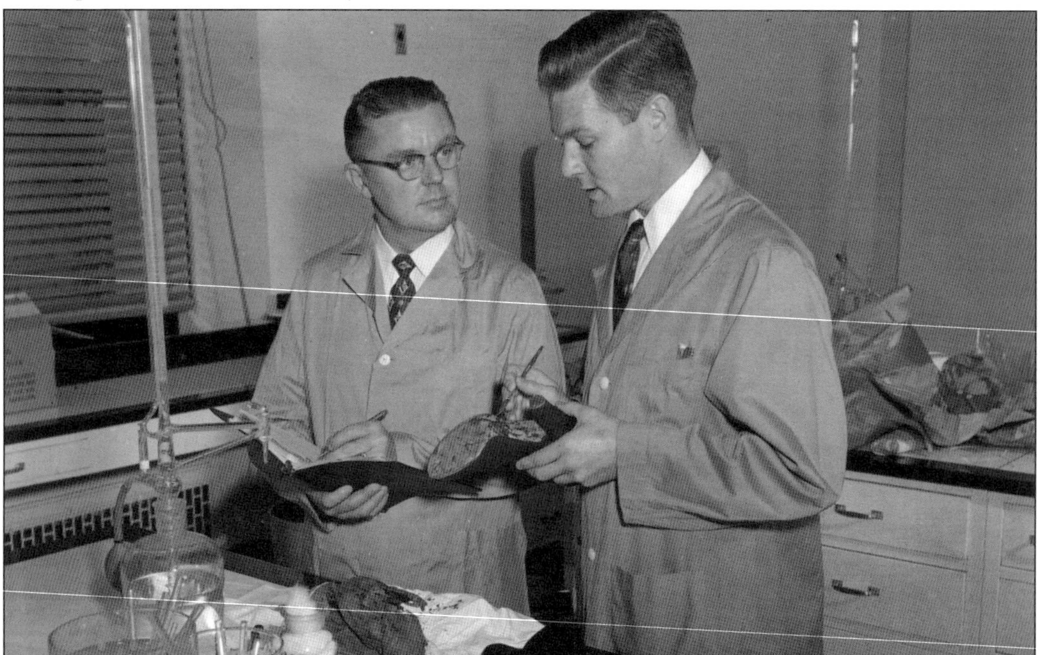

Educating the public on safety issues has been an important concern for the department through the decades. Above, in May 1965, Lt. Harvey Barnett (right) reviews several of the display boards that were used for demonstrations at the county fair and other civic functions with cadet officer John Moore (left). The displays covered the photographic history of the department, illegal weapons seized during criminal investigations, forms used by the department, communication aids, and in later years, with the increase of narcotics usage, a board showing those drugs was incorporated. Below, Sgt. Floyd Bedell (left) explains how one of the weapons functions, and the board behind him displays the forensic scientific aids used in the 1960s.

Part of the ongoing campaign to promote traffic safety had officers demonstrating the importance of seatbelt safety. The "Seatbelt Convincer" belonged to the Commonwealth of Virginia and traveled to various jurisdictions to aid in educational programs. Arlington County utilized the machine at schools and civic events in the county to educate young drivers and the general public of the importance of wearing a seatbelt during crashes. Officer Ed Redenbo (right) operates the machine while officer Romie Holmes observes the demonstration. An unidentified civilian is enduring the force of the machine during the demonstration. The other observers are not identified. (Photograph by Charles Adams.)

Forensic crime scene processing has gone through innumerable changes throughout the decades. From the 1940s through the 1960s, officers were assigned to the crime scene identification van. From the 1970s to the present, patrol officers at the rank of corporal (called agents) receive specialized training in latent fingerprint recovery, photography, and other means of collecting evidence at scenes. Cpl. Marc Hackett is recovering a latent fingerprint during an investigation. The processing kit he uses contains prints cards and various brushes to apply the different chemical powders in the kit that are used to recover prints from various surfaces. At present, there is a unit of officers trained in more complicated forensics evidence recovery, and they handle major crime scenes.

Cruiser design throughout the years changed, and the robot cruisers used as an educational tool to form relationships with children also changed in design. The robot cruisers have lights, sirens, and a decal that is the same as on the side of the cruisers used by patrol. The robot with the eyelashes displays the decal used on the patrol cars in the 1980s.

Deputy Chief Holl interacts with a group of youngsters surrounding the 1999 version of the robot cruiser. The siren and lights functioned, and the robot could be programmed to interact with the children and give safety tips. The children are holding McGruff coloring books, which the department routinely distributes at youth-related civic functions and the county fair, with additional safety tips.

Six

TRAFFIC AND SAFETY ENFORCEMENT

Arlington police have always supported campaigns against drinking and driving. From left to right, George Peever, Roxy Crack, and Roy Cornett pose on their motorcycles in December 1956 under a sign encouraging drivers not to drink and drive during the holidays. The department has continued with enforcement details, saturation enforcement, and check points, leading to a high percentage of arrests for alcohol-related offenses. (Courtesy of George Peever.)

In 1954, Sgt. Roxy Crack assists the fire department with traffic control at the scene of an accident at the intersection of Fort Myer Drive and Arlington Boulevard. (Courtesy of Shirley Crack.)

In 1955, Sgt. Roxy Crack is photographed standing next to his motorcycle on the center median, currently the location of High Occupancy Vehicle (HOV) lanes on Shirley Highway (Interstate 395). The Washington Gas and Light Company building is in the background. The building was recently demolished to make way for new construction. (Courtesy of Shirley Crack.)

Officer Warren Sisk (right) stands with motor officer Roxy Crack in 1953. The traffic safety bureau consisted of 10 motorcycle officers assigned to the day shift and three assigned to the evening shift. They had no radio communication, and the officers were required to use call boxes spread throughout the county. Helmets were not issued safety equipment. The duties of the officers comprised of writing tickets and providing escorts for funerals and special events. (Courtesy of Shirley Crack.)

Motor officers are, from left to right, Roxy Crack, John Kade, and Autry Mitchell, with Gordon Welch in the cruiser. Escorts often took dignitaries across the Potomac River into Washington, DC, as was the case here in 1953, in front of the Capitol. (Courtesy of Shirley Crack.)

The American Legion held their national convention in Washington, DC, on August 31, 1954, and the Arlington motor units were participants in the parade that crossed the intersection of North Fourteenth Street and Pennsylvania Avenue. (Courtesy of Shirley Crack.)

From left to right are Charles Murray, Autry Mitchell, George Peever, Roy Cornett, Roy Connors, Roxy Crack, Robert Weekly, John Kadel, Ray Cornett, Leroy Rasmussen, Bill Jeunette, Robert Jones, and Willard McArdle escorting Washington and Lee High School football players to the to the annual Old Oaken Bucket game on Thanksgiving Day 1954. Northern Virginia's toughest rivals would have a final contest, and the winner would claim the Old Oaken Bucket. (Courtesy of George Peever.)

In the early years, helmets were not part of the motor uniform, but concerns with safety brought about the implementation of them. Knee-high leather boots are custom designed for the individual wearer. Members of the motor unit in 1977 are, from left to right, Barry Laravie, James O'Connor, James Dodd, Robert Dexter, Lynn Davis, Robert Vogt, Chuck Boyer, Sgt. John Sidell, Phil Talbott, Lt. George Peever, and Neil Brennan. (Courtesy of George Peever.)

In 1982, motor officers stand in formation in front of the police building, 2100 North Fifteenth Street, used from the late 1970s to 1995. From left to right are, (first row) Lynn Davis, Michael Saupp, Cecil Nethers, and Phil Talbott; (second row) Maxie Jones, J.J. O'Connor, Gary Harris, and Keith Yoder.

The crossing guard unit in the 1960s promoted safety by providing pedestrian traffic control at intersections near elementary and middle schools. Crossing guards are still utilized today and provide safety in the proximity of the county's schools. (Courtesy of Barbara Jeunette.)

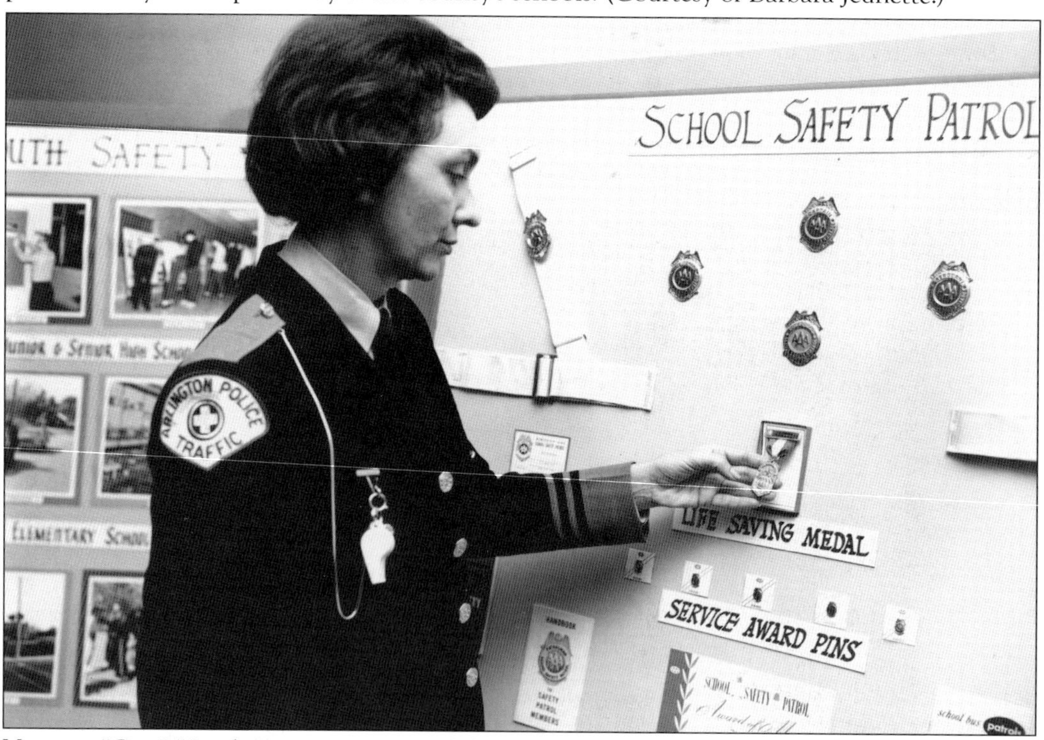

Virginia "Gigi" Henderson, supervisor of the crossing guard unit, looks at the display boards concerning pedestrian safety involving the youth of the community. School safety awards were given to safety patrols that assisted the crossing guards at school crossings. One of the awards that could be received was a life-saving award. (Courtesy of Barbara Jeunette.)

Since traffic control and safety enforcement are of great importance, officers are often recognized for outstanding performance in the education of enforcement efforts. On February 4, 1965, Inspector Walter Bell (left) and a Mr. Cave (president of Automotive Association) awarded officer Bill Jeunette a certificate and a savings bond for being named Safety Officer of the Year. Present-day officers continue to be recognized, and one of those awards is through Mothers Against Drunk Driving (MADD), given to the officer with the highest rate of driving while intoxicated (DWI) enforcement arrests and convictions. Educating the public about traffic safety was highlighted at a departmental open house in 1962. Below, Capt. Walter Bell shows Pat Garmany a map of the county with pins indicating accidents and fatalities during the year. (Above, courtesy of Barbara Jeunette.)

The annual Thanksgiving Day football game in 1953 required motor officers to assemble at the 1400 block of North Courthouse Road. They are, from left to right, Roy Cornett, George Peever, Roxy Crack, Autry Mitchell, Ernest Summers, John Kadel, unidentified, Bill Jeunette, Ray Cornett, and Willard McArdle. The intersection in the rear of the photograph is North Courthouse Road and Wilson Boulevard. The buildings to the immediate right make up the current criminal justice complex. Below, on New Year's Eve 1999, officers assemble at the same location as in 1953. From left to right are Kimberly Jones, David "Speedy" Gonzales, Bruce Silvernale, Richard Cox, Donald Grinder, Bruce Hackert, Mark Belanger, Mark DiGeronimo, Adam Stone, M. Jay Farr, and Mick Wenmoth. (Below, courtesy of Officer Adam Stone.)

Seven

Specialized Units

In 1984, Det. Jeff Steger of the crime resistance unit introduces McGruff the Crime Dog to Pres. Ronald Reagan for the first time by the invitation of the National Crime Prevention Coalition. (Photograph by Bill Fitz-Patrick, White House Photographer.)

Population growth in the county and the manpower demands of World War II that took so many of the regular members of the police force required the county to consider other options to supplement the department and continue to protect the citizens of the county. The auxiliary unit was created in 1942, and community volunteers were sworn in as air raid wardens to assist the police with new civil defense responsibilities. Their uniforms were khaki-colored pants, shirts, and hats, and they had patches or arm bands with a small shield design in a triangle within a circle. The members had training and annual inspections. The auxiliaries did not carry firearms, but they were armed with batons. Following the war, the uniform changed to blue, but the patches and badges were still different than that of sworn officers. Their duties began to focus on assisting with traffic and crowd control during special events.

There were no restrictions for becoming an auxiliary officer other than being of sound mind and good character. The unit was formed based on a person's desire to assist the community and to supplement the department during the war years. Age restrictions or physical abilities were not addressed. The units trained in a paramilitary atmosphere and can be seen lined up in formation with batons raised outside of the old courthouse building.

Patrol Camp began in the 1950s and was designed for fifth graders rising to sixth grade that were safety patrol captains. The camp was one week long, and 50 boys were sent to attend. The boys would learn the safest way to direct and stop traffic at intersections to assist younger children in crossing to school. The camp, located in Kilmarnock, Virginia, also offered the boys opportunities to participate in archery, boxing, softball, and nightly campfires. A veteran officer with the youth resources unit, Bill Jeunette, is seen at left in 1968 with Amos Finchum (left) and John Quade (right). In 1975, Officer Jeunette role plays at camp as "Chief Jeunette" with Officer Duling from Richmond, Virginia. Capt. Jim Daly, who currently serves with the department, was a camp participant in 1976. (Both, courtesy of Barbara Jeunette.)

Lt. Frank Palmer was a local radio and television personality in the 1950s. He implemented the department's campaign for traffic safety and was popular with children and adults. He had a large following, and while heading the department's safety bureau for four years, he had approximately 8,000 children join his 1-2-3 Go Club. The first safety television show aired February 22, 1950, on WTTG Channel 5 from 8:00 p.m. to 8:15 p.m., and it was among the first local television shows for kids. The program ran one evening each week from February 1950 to September 1954. Radio stations WEAM-AM 1390 and WARL-AM also featured Lieutenant Palmer, and he became a local hero. With his celebrity status, he introduced another local television hero, Captain Video and his Video Rangers, in the mid-1950s at Kann's Department Store located at North Fairfax Drive and North Kirkwood Road, the current location of the George Mason Law School. In 1951, at the Glebe Theater during a WEAM-AM radio remote, Palmer signs an autograph for one of his fans. (Courtesy of the Helen A. Palmer family archives.)

In the 1960s and 1970s, the motor unit was responsible for various duties, including traffic control, traffic enforcement, funeral and dignitary escorts, civil disturbance, and SWAT (special weapons and tactics) details. The unit participated in a mutual aid situation in October 1967 at the Pentagon, when approximately 55,000 demonstrators marched on the complex, protesting the Vietnam War. In October 1966, the unit monitored protesters promoting the racial integration of suburban apartment complexes. The scene escalated when members of the Klu Klux Klan and the American Nazi Party counter-demonstrated at the Buckingham complex. In 1971, the motor officers were involved with another war protest when demonstrators attempted to blockade the bridges connecting Washington, DC, with Arlington County, and more than 300 protesters were arrested. The motor unit also represented the department in parades and gatherings throughout Northern Virginia. On August 6, 1970, the unit participated at the US Navy Band Concert for the Young People. From left to right are officer Charles Boyer showing his motorcycle to an unidentified child, officer Tom "Patsy" Blake, and unidentified. (Photograph by Naval Photographic Center; courtesy of Charles Boyer.)

August 1958 brought the establishment of a civil disturbance unit. The officers were responsible for barricade situations, disasters, looking for missing children, and handling incidents associated with school integration. From left to right are Clyde Hall, John Sidell, Vernon Marsteller, and Rodney Mull being inspected by Lt. John Kadel and Sgt. Roy Lokey. Below, Sgt. Joe Heath hands out helmets and shotguns to, from left to right, unidentified, John Sidell, Vernon Marsteller, and Jim Stone. In 1967, the unit assisted with Vietnam War protestors at the Pentagon and civil rights demonstrations during the 1960s, when demonstrators refused to leave the Buckingham Community apartments protesting the lack of integration in housing. The American Nazi Party counter-demonstrated, and a number of clashes between protestors were quelled.

Officers John Kinney (center left) with Rommel and Ed Redenbo (center right) with Lucky became the first officers assigned to the K-9 unit established in December 1967. Roxy Crack (left) and Capt. Dudley Rector (right) were in charge of the unit. The formation of the unit allowed officers another means of capturing suspects with less lethal force. The dogs were specifically trained to use human scent to track fleeing suspects, locate evidence, and search buildings. Canine Rommel was stabbed while attempting to apprehend a burglary suspect at the Woodrow Wilson School at 1601 Wilson Boulevard. Rommel survived his injuries and returned to duty. At left, officer George Dooley and Ringo locate evidence left during a training exercise. (Left, courtesy of Rose Marie Dooley.)

The K-9 unit remains a support unit for the patrol division. The officers are responsible for regular patrol duties as well as working with their canine partners in locating suspects, evidence, and illegal narcotics, and some are trained to detect explosives. The unit participates in competitions and demonstrations at various public events. In the 2000s, officer Dan Gillenwater conducts a demonstration with his dog Sylvester the county fair.

To address the growing issue of gang-related crimes, the department formed a gang unit in 1998. The members attended training classes and conferences to keep apprised of the latest trends. Lt. Bruce Benson (left) attended the fourth anti-gang (anti-bandia) conference in El Salvador in 2008; he is pictured here with a lieutenant from the Policia Nacional Civil. (Courtesy of Lt. Bruce Benson.)

The 1960s and 1970s brought a change to the department, and resources were allocated to form the youth resource unit as an outreach program to youth in the community. The unit supervised a summer patrol camp and worked in conjunction with the county school system. Members of the unit are, from left to right, (first row) Tom Baird, Delores Brown, Bill Jeunette, Jean Balge, and Gary Hamric; (second row) Steve Clevenger, John Moore, Irving Comer, Jim Stone, and Guy Clark. In December 31, 1967, Irving Comer was hired, the first African American officer with the department. The county to that date had received few applications from African Americans, and those that had applied did not meet qualifications. Delores Brown was the first sworn female officer, and John Moore had been a member of the cadet program.

The department has always looked for new ways to educate the community about crimes and how to not become a victim. To promote crime resistance, the officers worked with the Hecht Company located in the Parkington Shopping Center (now Macy's at Ballston Commons Mall) in the 1970s. The store had a wall of large windows, and a campaign sign promoting crime resistance was posted with high visibility from the intersection of Wilson Boulevard and North Glebe Road. The crime resistance unit conducted security checks of residences and businesses. Suggestions would be offered as to how to better secure homes, businesses, and vehicles. The hope was that with better security there would be lower crime statistics. Citizens were encouraged to engrave identification numbers on valuables and record serial numbers to assist in recovering stolen property.

In another youth outreach program, officers participate in a basketball game with residents of the Hall's Hill neighborhood in the north section of Arlington. Members of the team are, from left to right, Chad Ramsey, Pat Donahue, Sean Carrig, James "Matt" Smith, Steve Meincke, and Robert Jacobs. Chief Flynn is observing in the background.

Det. Bill Golab explains methods of preventing auto theft and larceny of valuables from vehicles to a citizen at the Arlington County Fair in August 1999. The unit promoted locking devices and window etching with the vehicle identification number. Several units within the police department have displays at the fair to promote safety and community relations.

Parking aides are used throughout the county to ensure that parking violations are enforced, and tickets are written for those who break the law. The aides are assigned to certain areas, and many cover the areas on foot, but some are assigned vehicles or scooters. Assisting with traffic control at special events is another function of the unit. Parking tickets have historically been written on carbonized paper, but in recent years, a small handheld computer prints out the information entered on the key pad. In 2000, the unit was supervised by Sgt. Ron Paquin (center left) and Lt. Roy Austin (center right). Prior to meter enforcement, tires were chalked to keep track of the length of time a vehicle was left parked in a space. Det. Tom Bell demonstrates how parking aides driving Cushmans would chalk a tire.

In an effort to address the increases in street robberies in the mid-1970s, a plainclothes unit (robbery task force) was formed. It transitioned to the operations task force (OTF), and the unit primarily addressed the increasing number of burglaries. In the early 1980s, the OTF was became the tactical unit. Members pictured here are, from left to right, (first row) Doug Hearn and John Mitchell; (second row) Lowell Toliver, Kevin Norwood, Gary Davis, John McCarthy, and Sgt. Chuck Gavin; (third row) John Cook, Joe Marchi, Doug Miller, and Al Pola. The unit continued to evolve with crime trends, and the increase of crimes involving narcotics was dealt with by the squad as well as robberies, burglaries, and sexual assaults. Officers assigned in the 1990s are, from left to right, Matt Yonkers, Cheryl Nordstrom, Tom Goldman, Mike Baker, Darrell Abate, Troy Newenhouse, and Wayne Vincent.

During his tenure with the department, Chief Flynn brought with him the concept of community policing. He empowered officers to utilize teamwork to solve situations they noticed created criminal activity. From left to right are Cindy Garcia, Kip Malcom, and Henry Buchhofer, meeting after roll call to review a map produced by the research and development section to track criminal incidents in a certain area. Part of the problem-solving concept was to use CPTED (crime prevention through environmental design). Officers would review crimes that had occurred and then look to see what could be changed with landscaping, lighting, and structures to see if something could be done to change the environment and make it less appealing for criminals. The bicycle unit was also utilized, and the unit officers gave the appearance of being more approachable to the public. Officer Kip Malcolm shows his bicycle to a youngster during a street festival.

The special weapons and tactics unit (SWAT) relies on a teamwork concept. The team's movements must be performed in coordination with each other for purposes of quickness of movement and for safety. Officers demonstrating the team movement are, from left to right, Viet Nguyen, Marc Hackett, and Robert Jones. Another component of the SWAT team is the crisis negotiations team. The officers of that team are part-time members, as are the officers on the tactical team. The negotiators train on a monthly basis to check equipment and practice active listening skills. The team is assigned a van that houses the equipment and is used as the negotiations center during incidents. Det. Richard Schoemb uses a bullhorn during a training exercise in an attempt to make contact with a subject.

Pictured here in 1903 are the businesses along Rosslyn's North Moore Street, just prior to commonwealth attorney Crandall Mackey's raid with his Good Citizens League on the illegal saloons and brothels. Following the raid, in an effort to clean up the area, a sign was posted at the north end of North Moore Street stating a $50 fine for dumping in the county. In 2014, that fine amount would equate to a $1,300 fine. (Courtesy of the Center for Local History, Arlington County Public Library.)

The 1950s and 1960s brought an economic upsurge to the Rosslyn area, seen here on North Moore Street and Lee Highway, and more commercial and residential development started. To stay in pace with crime that increases with changes in the population and the economic environment, the department increased from a force of 79 officers to 172. The increase in housing was to accommodate government workers, and the county also saw the construction of one of the first large regional retail shopping center in the nation, Parkington Shopping Center, now Ballston Commons Mall.

In 1937, the rural characteristics of the county are evident with this view of Washington, DC, taken from the east end of Columbia Pike around the area of South Orme Street. A cow can be seen grazing in the field in the front. The open fields on the far side of the houses are the current locations for the Pentagon and the Pentagon City Mall.

This 1962 aerial view of Rosslyn at North Lynn Street and North Nineteenth Street looking toward the District of Columbia show the saloon district of the early 1900s transitioning to an industrial commercial district. The 1965 view of Crystal City and the vacant fields where the Pentagon City Mall now stands also demonstrates that with a changing environment, the department had to change to keep up with the increased population. The department of the 1960s totaled 172 officers, each with a salary of $4,900. Present-day officers total 370 with a base salary of $48,000. They serve a population of approximately 225,000. Arlington has a land area of 26 square miles, which includes military bases, Arlington Cemetery, and the airport.

Eight

Significant Events

Lt. Roxy Crack demonstrates traffic control in front of the old Lansburg department store in Shirlington Village to a visiting policewoman from Israel in 1959. The department had gained international recognition for their training program, and officers from Korea, Turkey, Jordan, South America, Iceland, Afghanistan, Indonesia, and Vietnam came to learn police policies and procedures. (Courtesy of Shirley Crack.)

Pictured here in 1950 are, from left to right, John Kadel, Harold Carr, Roxy Crack, Russell Moller, and Charlie Wood as they pretend to arrest Abbott and Costello during a playful meeting. Abbott and Costello appeared at the Freedom Fair at Wilson Boulevard and North Glebe Road in Ballston. The fair featured appearances by personalities of the era and was held in honor of the 15th anniversary of the US saving bonds. Below, Walter Winchell, an actor, writer, and a very powerful and feared radio commentator and gossip columnist, made an appearance with, from left to right, Roxy Crack, Roy Cornett, and John Kadel. (Below, photograph by Bill Little.)

On February 2, 1959, Stratford Junior High School (now H-B Woodlawn High School), located at 4100 Vacation Lane, became the first public secondary school in Virginia to be integrated. Four African American seventh graders began school with over 100 officers in riot gear assigned to the civil disturbance unit standing by. The transition was smooth, and there was no violence that day. Officers stood by the next day just to make sure that nothing violent occurred.

Several local and out-of-state departments participated in a shooting competition at Lorton, Virginia, in June 1957. Arlington accumulated 19 medals and three trophies. Two trophies were team awards for first place in .22-caliber and .38-caliber competition. The medals were for various placements in the overall competition, including two first places in individual shooting for Officers Hall and Pope. Members of the team competing are, from left to right, Pvt. William Hall, Lt. Ernest Summers, Pvt. Raymond Pope, and Sgt. Roxy Crack. Officer Hall received a trophy for having the grand point aggregate.

Sporting activities have been popular with members of the department. The police baseball team competed locally and is pictured here in front of the Washington and Lee High School in 1949. Team members are, from left to right, (first row) Raymond Cole, three unidentified players, Elmer Redmon, Walter Coppage, Emett McLane, unidentified, and Gilbert Stream; (second row) Bernie Lunsford, unidentified, John Wise, Bernard Keyes, Ernest Miller, Dudley Rector, Douglas Topley, Walter Bell, J. Crissman, and Russell Runyon.

In September 1981, the racing team won the first annual police chase race held at Fort Harrison, Richmond Battlefield. Steve Gunzenhauser (first row, left) took first place individual, and Steve Holl (first row, right) holds the first place team trophy. Other members of the team are, from left to right, (second row) Frank Carver, Paul Kozich, and Greg Brewer.

On November 17, 1963, three of the 69 male inmates housed in the jail overpowered two deputies. One of the subjects jumped a deputy and took his keys. When another deputy came to check on him, one of the subjects struck him. The deputies retreated, locking themselves with other inmates in a cell for protection. One of the escapees took a revolver from a cabinet and yelled "Jailbreak." A woman passing by heard this and ran into the police department to report the incident. Sgt. Truman Adams, Lt. Harvey Barnett, and Privates Carey Cole and Philip Nielson responded to the third floor of the jail. They deployed tear gas, at which time one of the escapees fired three rounds from the revolver at them. The escapes then retreated to the women's cellblock. After negotiations with a megaphone, the escapees broke a window and threw the gun out. They surrendered by climbing out a window with the use of a ladder supplied by the fire department. The jail facility was surrounded by 50 Arlington County police officers, 10 Virginia state troopers, and numerous firemen.

In 1985, the crime resistance unit took advantage of technology and developed a community services unit using the media. The members had a televised show that would address citizens' concerns and educate the public with ongoing trends in crime prevention. Some members of the unit were bilingual, and this helped bridge language and cultural barriers between the department and an increasing Hispanic immigrant population. From left to right are Detectives Greg Kurasz, Tom Bell, and Robert Kirschner on the television set. The map of Arlington County in the background shows the different neighborhood boundaries. Det. James Badey, who had served in Vietnam, became a liaison officer with the Vietnamese community because of his knowledge of the language and their customs. Much of the Clarendon section had businesses operated by Vietnamese immigrants, and there was an increasing problem with Asian gangs.

To create a closer association with the community, the first Citizen's Police Academy was established in 1998. The curriculum was organized by Sgt. Regina Heising, who was in charge of the training unit. The curriculum was designed to allow the participants an overview of the department and how it functions. The 13-week (one night, each week) classes were taught by officers from different sections of the department and covered subjects from recruiting, training, patrol, traffic, and investigative functions to firearms and SWAT. The program was favorably covered by the media and helped the rapport between the community and the department. Participants ranged from businesspeople to community leaders, with some taking volunteer positions within the department following the program. Participant Larry Tingle (father of officer Aaron Tingle) was one of the police department chaplains.

Providing security and traffic control for special events places demands on staffing from several units within the department. Officers from traffic, patrol, SWAT, investigations, and the parking aide unit work several large events each year. Those events include community festivals, the county fair, Fourth of July fireworks viewing from the Iwo Jima Memorial in Rosslyn, and the Marine Corps Marathon. The Marine Corps Marathon is held the final Sunday every October. The marathon begins and ends in Arlington and has been held here since its inception in 1976. The race is the third largest in the United States, and 30,000 runners with hundreds of thousands of spectators participate. The race is led off the starting line by motor officers to make sure the race course is clear.

Officers have always been encouraged to bolster relations between the community and the department. Officer Keith Bryan talks to several youngsters in the late 1970s at the Lucky 7 convenience store on Shirlington Road in the Green Valley section of the Nauck community. Nauck is the oldest African American neighborhood in Arlington; it was a stopping place during the migration from the South to the North after the Civil War. Recently freed slaves from Freedman's Village (now Arlington National Cemetery) bought subdivided lots from John Nauck, who owned 46 acres in 1874. The relations between the residents of Nauck and the police have at times been rough and have resulted in several confrontations. The area had increased patrols and enforcement action with the increase of the drug trade in the 1970s and 1980s. The uniform Officer Bryan is wearing consisted of a light blue shirt and dark pants with a stripe to match the shirt color.

Officers carry the body of John Carl Parks after he was slain on January 20, 1954. Earlier that day, Parks shot and killed Det. Russell Pettie, who had responded to the suspect's residence at 1808 North Taylor Street to serve a warrant for a mental detention hearing. Several jurisdictions responded to the scene, and after expending approximately 7,000 rounds of ammunition, Parks was killed after barricading himself in the attic. The officers are, from left to right, Walter Kadel (on the ladder), Ernest Summers, John Kadel, unidentified, Dudley Rector, and Alvin Fuchsman. Officer Roxy Crack is standing in front of the porch.

Public access to information is a function of the public information office, formed in the late 1970s. The public information officer (PIO) at present is a civilian employee, Dustin Sternbeck. The office liaises with various media sources: television, radio, and print. The department's website features crime reports, traffic information, wanted subjects, and information on how to contact the department. The office runs various programs to support community involvement. A recent project was the first Chief-for-a-Day contest, in which participants wrote essays on the topic of what it means to be a police officer. The winner was nine-year-old Patrick Omberg (at left), and he was sworn in as chief on August 4, 2014. Below, Chief Omberg poses with his officers; from left to right are Mick Wenmoth, Kip Malcolm, Cheryl Nordstrom with Drago, and Richard Cox. The project was managed by a student intern, Jessica Grisler. Student interns from various universities are utilized throughout the department in various sections.

Nine

INVESTIGATIONS

Det. Kenny Adams (left) and Det. Bob Carrig review composite drawings in 1980 concerning a suspect wanted in a brutal attack on an elderly woman in the northern section of the county. The victim was attacked in her home and was discovered barely alive under items that the suspect stacked on top of her believing she was dead. The suspect was apprehended and convicted.

On May 8, 1941, Bolivian captain Alberto Taborga, military aide to the Bolivian president, was injured in a plane crash at Washington Airport (Reagan National). The pilot, Capt. Rafael Rivas, was killed. The plane, a Beech 17 Staggerwing, was on a goodwill flyover from New York to La Paz, Bolivia. The Bolivian minister, Dr. Luis Guachalla, watched the plane fly to 100 feet and burst into flames when it struck the ground. Pictured here surveying the damage are, from left to right, C. Burns Pressley, Minister Guachalla, Hugh Jones, John Sanders, Jack Ward, and Douglas Topley. Officers responded to another crash scene on January 13, 1982, when an Air Florida flight crashed into the Fourteenth Street Bridge and plunged into the Potomac River. Frigid temperatures caused the wings to ice, and the plane struck seven vehicles on the bridge, killing four people as well as 73 passengers. Six survivors were rescued from the river. Arlington assisted Washington Metropolitan Police, who had primary jurisdiction.

On December 10, 1958, an accident occurred at the intersection of Columbia Pike and Washington Boulevard following a vehicle pursuit. The pursuit started at Columbia Pike and South Oakland Street. The subject lost control, struck three cars, and flipped the van he was driving. He drove up the embankment, ran across Washington Boulevard and into a culvert leading onto the grounds of Fort Myer. He was apprehended and held for mental observation. The courts declared him incompetent to stand trial. (Courtesy of Barbara Jeunette.)

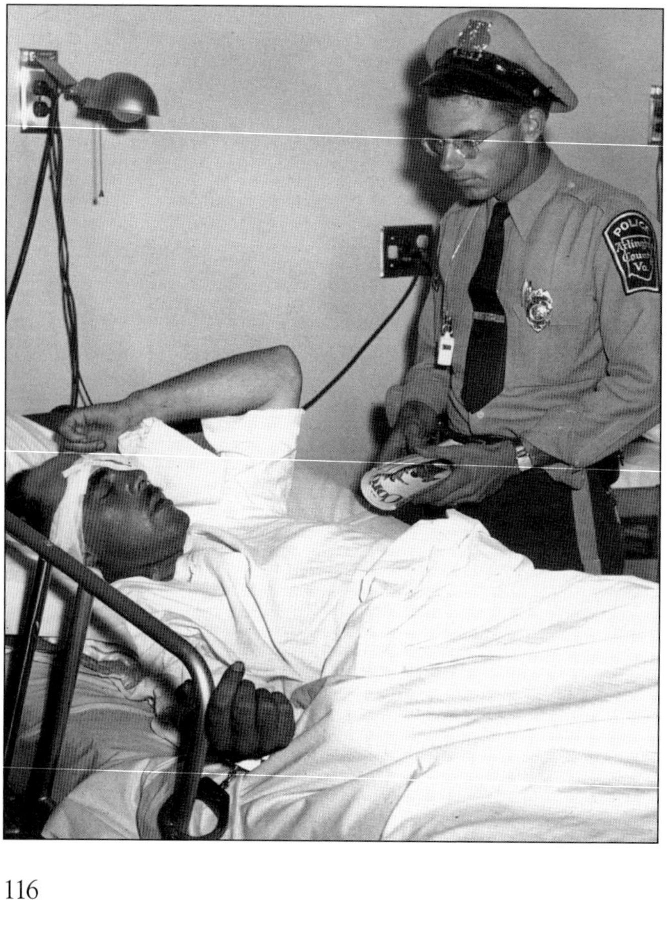

Traffic enforcement and safety has always a priority within the department. Enforcement of speed and drunk driving infractions were generally the source of most tickets issued or arrests made. Officer Bill Jeunette surveys damage at the scene of an accident at North Twenty-third Street and Old Dominion Drive on June 12, 1953, where a new Oldsmobile collided with a fuel oil truck belonging to the A.P. Woodson Company located at the 6800 block of Lee Highway. Jeunette is pictured at left at Arlington Hospital interviewing a handcuffed suspect that was with another subject wanted by the FBI. The pair attempted to go around a roadblock at approximately 100 miles per hour and crashed at South Glebe and Old Glebe Roads. (Both, courtesy of Barbara Jeunette.)

From left to right are Walter Kadel, unidentified, Bill Jeunette, Hal Burchette, suspect Richard L. McCaughey, Det. Russell Runyon, and suspect John Kensinger at the scene of a homicide where the suspects had robbed a cab driver of $22. Kensinger shot the driver in the back of the head. McCaughey was sentenced to 12 years, and Kensinger pled guilty. He was electrocuted on May 26, 1954. McCaughey and Kensinger were traveling magazine salesmen from Chicago, Illinois, brought to Arlington for sales.

In 1953, the detective bureau was assigned many cases that needed follow-up. Those cases included homicides, robberies, assaults, burglaries, and thefts. Each detective had his own desk in a shared room; clockwise from left are Charles Lee, George Coppage, Robert Weekly, Lt. John Sanders, Billy Hammer, and secretary Mildred Drake.

Interviewing victims and handling evidence are regular duties of the detective bureau. In 1956, Detectives Jackey Snoots (left) and Chuck Mackey (right) interview a victim of a criminal incident at a convenience store where the clerk was assaulted by a subject that used a piece of a wooden pole as a weapon, striking the clerk on the left side of his face. Below, Det. Sonny Lee looks at tagged evidence bags and hubcaps on his desk in the bureau.

Arlington police were informed on May 28, 1956, that teenaged "greasers" were going to be involved in a robbery and riot at the Arlington Forest Shopping Center at Arlington Boulevard and North Park Drive. The results of that information lead to the arrests of 27 boys. Detectives Walter Kadel (left) and William Dinsmore (right) show some of the weapons that were confiscated. A decade later, another confrontation would take place at the Safeway in the Lee Harrison Shopping Center on Lee Highway and North Harrison Street. The report was that 200 Pagan motorcycle members were going to shoot members of the Avengers gang. The members came armed with 25-mm automatics, brass knuckles, AR-15 assault rifles, bats, and clubs studded with nails. Officers were legally barred by state law from intervening until shots were fired, but once the shooting started, the officers converged with Thompson submachine guns. The only injury was a ricochet injuring a state trooper, and 18 gang members were arrested.

George Lincoln Rockwell, the founder and leader of the American Nazi Party, was assassinated after leaving the Econowash Laundromat at the Dominion Hills Shopping Center on the 5900 block of Wilson Boulevard. Two rounds went through the windshield of his 1958 Chevrolet. Rockwell staggered from the vehicle and pointed toward the roof before collapsing on the pavement. The gunman ran along the roofline, jumped to the ground, and was located at a bus stop. The suspect, John Patler, an expelled member of the group, was recognized by Inspector Raymond Cole, who was familiar with the organization. Patler was convicted, sentenced to two years, and paroled in 1975. The Nazi headquarters was located at 928 North Randolph Street, until Rockwell established his "Stormtrooper" barracks at 6150 Wilson Boulevard in the Dominion Hills area. The house has been demolished and is now part of the Upton Hills Regional Park. Following Rockwell's death, the party moved its headquarters to 2507 North Franklin Road (now the Java Shack). Det. Walter Hughes is standing in front of the victim's vehicle with an unidentified motor officer.

Officers are, from left to right, unidentified, Francis "Tony" Beakes, and Det. George Peever carrying the 7.63-mm C-96 Mauser "Broomhandle" semiautomatic used by John Patler to ambush George Lincoln Rockwell, leader of the American Nazi Party. The weapon was recovered in about six inches of water, buried under rocks below a wooden foot bridge in Four Mile Run Creek in Bon Air Park.

Det. Walter Kadel looks into the 1958 Chevrolet owned by George Lincoln Rockwell. Rockwell had just entered the vehicle on August 25, 1967, when two shots pierced the windshield. Rockwell slumped over the steering wheel and then fell out onto the pavement at the Dominion Hills Shopping Center.

Ten

Pentagon Attack Response

September 11, 2001, was a day that will live forever in memories of the officers that worked that day and the weeks that followed. Arlington County Police were responsible for the initial scene stabilization, traffic control, and perimeter security. Officers are, from left to right, Henry Buchhofer, Richard Cox (who observed American Airlines Flight 77 hit the Pentagon at 9:37 a.m.), Deputy Chief Steve Holl, and Cecelia Ashe.

Officers hearing the news responded to the county to assist, and they worked tirelessly on security details in addition to their regular shifts. Sgt. Jim Daly and Lt. Brian Berke were assigned to the staffing command at Firehouse No. 5 in Crystal City to coordinate manpower resources from other surrounding agencies with Arlington's. The black band worn on their badges was worn by every officer to honor those that had fallen. Bands are commonly worn when an officer has died in the line of duty, but here it was to mourn all victims of this terrorist act.

Chief Flynn and Deputy Chief Holl were both absent from the department on business. Commanding officers present in the county assumed control until their return and assigned responding officers to security details and to the 38 traffic posts to help ease the flow of traffic fleeing the area. Deputy Chief Holl (right) is seen upon his return, and motor officer Adam Stone assists with perimeter security.

Perimeter security continued to be a high priority in the days that followed. Canines were used to check any suspicious packages that may be found in the area. Canine officer Dave Torpy patrols the perimeter near Interstate 395 and the south parking area of the Pentagon with his partner Brook. Officer Susan Noack watches as Cpl. Joe Peralta searches a bag belonging to a subject, found sitting along the security fence. In the days following, personnel were reassigned from traffic and security details to evidence recovery. Rotating teams of 20 officers searched the debris fields located in the north parking area, attempting to locate documents, personal items, plane parts, and human remains.

An additional command center was set up within the confines of the Pentagon property. The department's mobile command bus (outfitted with computers and phones) and tents were set up at the scene to have a closer point for command staff to make assignments and coordinate personnel. The south parking area of the Pentagon is seen in the background with numerous tents and trucks. Several business, including eateries, barbers, chiropractors, and masseuses both local and national responded, making a tent city to assist the first responders. At left, Det. Darrin Cassidy attaches the American flag to the command tent.

Perimeter security on Washington Boulevard was heightened on September 12, 2001, where unidentified officers are standing adjacent to the crash scene awaiting the arrival of Pres. George W. Bush and Secretary of Defense Donald Rumsfeld to survey the damage. Below, members of the Special Weapons and Tactics Team are, from left to right, Daniel Murphy, Viet Nguyen, Bruce Benson, unidentified, and Greg Sloan (with back turned), part of the team responsible to maintaining the security at the perimeter of the Pentagon property.

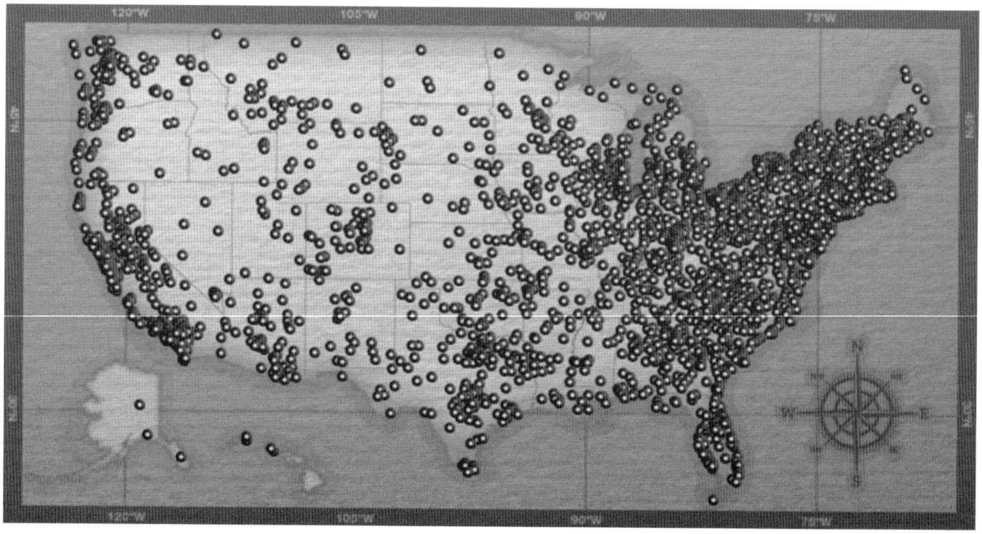